The Sociology of Education: Introductory Analytical Perspectives

by D. F. Swift

*Institute of Education,
University of Oxford*

LONDON

ROUTLEDGE & KEGAN PAUL

NEW YORK: HUMANITIES PRESS

First published 1969
by Routledge & Kegan Paul Ltd
Broadway House, 68–74 Carter Lane
London, E.C.4
Reprinted 1969

Printed in Great Britain
by Willmer Brothers Limited
Birkenhead, Cheshire

SBN 7100 6360 1 (c)

SBN 7100 6362 8 (p)

General editor's introduction

Today sociology is going through a phase of great expansion. Not only is there a widespread general interest in the subject, but there is a rapid growth in the numbers of new courses at Universities, Colleges of Education and elsewhere. As a result there is an increasing number of potential readers of introductory textbooks. Some will be motivated by general interest; some will want to find out enough about the subject to see whether they would like to pursue a formal course in it; and others will already be following courses into which an element of sociology has been fused. One approach to these readers is by means of the comprehensive introductory volume giving a general coverage of the field of sociology; another is by means of a series of monographs each providing an introduction to a selected topic. Both these approaches have their advantages and disadvantages. The *Library of Sociology* adopts the second approach. It will cover a more extensive range of topics than could be dealt with in a single volume; while at the same time each volume will provide a thorough introductory treatment of any one topic. The reader who has little or no knowledge in the field will find within any particular book a foundation upon which to build, and to extend by means of the suggestions for further reading.

Education is today the centre of controversy among teachers, parents, politicians, and educators themselves The extent and intensity of this controversy bears witness to the importance of education as a process in society. This importance is derived partly from the fact that it is through educational processes and institutions that knowledge and skills as well as native talents are developed. It is necessary for the members of a society to be clear about what they expect from their educational institutions; different kinds of society will require different kinds of skill and knowledge to be imparted as a basis for citizenship and to provide manpower for changing occupational patterns. Unfortunately clarity of thought in these matters is by no means always apparent.

A second source of controversy arises from the different life chances which stem from the possession of different amounts of education. Thus arguments about education, whatever the terms in which they are carried on, always contain a reference either implicit or explicit to the way the particular society is stratified.

Education is also concerned with the development of values and personality, and here also there is difference of opinion as to what these values should be, and how different educational procedures affect personality development.

Finally, the educational process is carried on both through the formal institutions of education, such as schools, universities, or youth clubs, and through less formal groupings such as the family or the peer group.

There is no shortage of literature in this very important field, nor is statistical material in short supply. But one often feels that more heat than light is generated in discussions on education because of a failure to see the educational process as a whole in relation to its society. This Dr. Swift attempts to do for the student. His discussion is set within a specifically sociological frame of reference, and his first two chapters are devoted largely to a development of this framework. He then proceeds through a discussion of the school as an organisation to the social environment surrounding the school and finally to a consideration of some of the basic issues concerning the functions of education for society.

The reader may be surprised to find little description of the structure of the British educational system. Clearly, any theoretical statements made are of little value unless they can be shown to apply to real situations. However, with so much ground to cover. Dr. Swift has chosen to collect the relevant empirical material into a source book to which the interested reader may make reference.

A. R. EMERSON

Contents

1
Sociology and education

Introduction

Modern society is generating a great demand for all kinds
of social scientists to put their knowledge and skills at the
service of society. We are finding less use for the amateur
and we believe we have greater need for the expert. Since
many of our problems are social, one kind of expert we
turn to is the sociologist.

But pleas for help do not always bring a satisfactory
response from the sociologist. The layman usually expects
too much or misconceives the kind of contribution sociology can make. In the long run the interests of sociologist
and social problem-solver overlap because if sociology is
to help in solving problems of society it will have to be done
well. In the short run, however, we can expect some conflict and much misunderstanding.

By his own standards, the sociologist may not always
be equipped to help in dealing with social problems, but
under the urgent pressure of events he has become more

involved in them. In the process he has begun to acquire a certain measure of confidence that sociological thinking and information-collecting skills are sufficiently improved to be relevant.

One area of the discipline which illustrates this developing confidence is the sociology of education. During the last decade in Britain the sociologist has begun to play a part in the statutory administrative system as consultant, administrator and researcher. At the same time the findings of research are being assimilated into the folklore of teaching at what, given the small amount of research, may even be thought to be a dangerous speed.

A minor revolution in our attitudes towards education is resulting. Instead of looking upon it as a form of national expenditure we are beginning to think of it as one of the more financially fruitful kinds of capital investment. Partly as a result, education is becoming looked upon as a means for producing talent rather than a sorting and selecting system for finding it. This book aims to exemplify that way of looking at social life which is helping to encourage the development of such a fundamental change in our view of education. It offers a set of conceptual models based upon the sociological perspective.

The sociology of education

Until recently sociology of education dealt with social improvement. For example, Durkheim the father of modern 'educational sociology', as it was usually called, was deeply disturbed by the developing trends in modern industrial society. He sought a way out from approaching disaster by re-organising social life, and education was to provide the solution. (Durkheim 1956). At the present time we have similar examples from many developing countries where deliberate programmes of community development work have usually been started with the explicit intention of raising living standards by influencing the attitudes of its inhabitants. This is often a massive project in adult education which must be based upon sociological knowledge in so far as its aims and its means are social.

It would be wrong to suggest that this belief in the rôle of education is a new one which follows solely from the findings of sociology. The notion that we can improve society through deliberate action on the process of education is implicit in much theorising about education. Plato's plan for a proper balance in the perceived conflict between the individual's drive for personal excellence and the claim of the state upon his actions implicitly assumed that education could be so arranged as to facilitate an optimum arrangement. The sociology of education since Durkeim has developed through the insights which socio-psychological theory and research brought to our understanding of the social nature of man. For example, in conjunction with his educational scheme, Plato bequeathed us some ideas about the intractability of human intelligence and the likelihood of specialisation of interest. They have been fundamental in shaping Western European education but modern research is showing them to be erroneous. On the other hand, Durkeim's desire to save and remake his society led to proposals which were based upon a sounder understanding of the social process than that usually shown by earlier philosophers who tended to base their theories upon their intuitive 'understanding' of individual psychology.

It is obvious that the study of education can make a valuable contribution, both to sociology and to society. The next step is to ask how the best interests of sociologist, educator and administrator can be served in the process.

3

In the first place, the answer must be that the sociologist should do good sociology. That is, he must work according to the rules of his discipline. But in doing so he will run the risk of providing answers which are inappropriate or undesirable in the eyes of the educator.

Taylor (1967) has suggested that separate use of two terms, 'educational sociology' and 'the sociology of education' might be maintained in order to preserve the distinction between an emphasis upon educational or social problems and an emphasis upon sociological problems. For Taylor

> although in its more rigorous forms it [educational sociology] has brought a good deal of sociological insight to bear upon educational problems, it has tended to be hortatory rather then empirical, inspirational rather than objective, and synoptic rather than analytic. (Taylor, 1967, p. 191)

It is useful to look upon education as standing in a relationship to sociology similar to that held by engineering in relation to physics. It is the technology to the pure science. Practitioners take the knowledge and theories evolved by the pure scientists and apply them to the solution of practical problems. As a matter of fact the relationship also works in the opposite direction, because solving practical problems also contributes to knowledge, but that does not alter the analytical usefulness of the distinction.

Since the difference lies in the *reason* for carrying out the research in the first place it is of no practical importance. The intention is 'pure' when the research is carried out in order to improve our knowledge of how society works or of the methods by which we can arrive at valid information about it. On the other hand the reason for applied research is a desire or a commission to solve some specific

4

problem of society as perceived by a client. There is a distinction, but only a conceptual one, between research for sociology and research for society.

The point is that one can (and almost all sociologists do) hope that sociology will be of help to society without making the patently erroneous stipulation that whenever we do sociology we should be actually trying to solve one of society's problems.

One of the important aims for the physical and biological sciences is to bring about changes which are intended. Similarly, prediction and control are aims of social science. The way to test the validity of social science knowledge is to predict changes that occur either without intervention of the sociologist or because of it. If it occurs because of intervention we might say that it is engineered. This is exactly what education seeks to do, both for the individual, and through him, the society. In a very real sense the application of social or behavioural science is a necessary (though not sufficient) aspect of education.

So much for what sociology contributes to education. We also need to look at what education offers sociology. If sociology is to progress as a genuine science it must become more 'experimental'. The system of education offers situations in which experiments are possible without offending our own values about human beings. In doing so it provides sociology with an opportunity to meet the challenge of what many people consider to be the vital requirements of science—the ability to predict and organise social change. Sociological research in education, therefore, is simply experimental or observational sociology.

The development of the discipline (and hence its value in society) follows from a mutually stimulating relationship between theorising and information-gathering each of which is dependent upon the other for its meaning. There is no point in distinguishing between the motives for doing the research. What matters is the candlepower of the theories which illuminate the information and the rigour with which it is collected. Consequently sociology and education have a great deal to offer each other.

Sociological approaches to problems

The theories, concepts and research methods of sociology offer one set of tools for thinking about education. These are different from other ways of approaching it. For example, an ethical point of view is different in all three elements whereas a psychological one would differ much less radically. However, the difference in perspective can cause a very great deal of controversy between people who are employing the different perspectives without realising it (Swift 1965 b). The one point which must be made clear at the outset is that we cannot claim a superior position for the sociological perspective. It is simply one way of looking at education which will add to our understanding of it, but it cannot replace an ethical or a psychological view.

The special contribution of sociology arises from its interest in the structure and functioning of *groups* varying in size from two people to a nation. Instead of looking at human behaviour as the actions of individuals it looks for the regularities and similarities in behaviour which are referable to a group context. The discipline assumes that one valid way of explaining the action of human beings is to think of it as a product of their social experience. The consequences of this contentious-sounding, but thoroughly innocuous, statement will be dealt with in later chapters. For the time being, it is enough to say that the patterns which can be seen in social behaviour are usually the result of group membership. Consequently, in analysing them we are describing the structure and functioning of social groups.

There are two kinds of perspective, therefore, from which we can view social behaviour—the individual and the group perspective. Because we are so used to individuals as concrete things we find it easy to talk in terms of the individual level of abstraction. On the other hand, because the group is not a concrete thing we often find it a difficult idea to deal with despite the many group level abstractions to be found in everyday thinking about society. Ideas like 'the team' 'the motherland' and 'the economy' are attempts at sociological thinking. Through many years of practice, we tend to look upon action as the result of the motives, desires and intentions of the actors. This is a valid way of doing it, but not the only valid way. The sociological perspective points towards the ways in which the actor arrived at these motives, desires and intentions and at the pressures which direct and constrain action.

Neither the individual level nor the group level abstraction is analytically superior. They should go hand in hand, giving complementary explanations for social situations. Educators need to use both perspectives if they are to plan their activities effectively. The sociology of education, in describing the group processes to which individuals are subjected and the influence of one group upon another, provides an understanding of the context within which the aims of education are pursued. The individual perspective deals with whatever a person brings into that context and the means by which he assimilates his experience of it.

What is education?

As far as the sociologist is concerned, education is something which takes place in society because of three basic facts about the human race. Firstly, everything which comprises the way of life of a society or group of people is learned. Nothing of it is biologically inherited. Secondly, the human infant is incredibly receptive to experience. By this we mean that he is capable of developing a wide range of beliefs about the world around him, skills in manipulating it and values as to how he should manipulate it. Thirdly, this infant is also totally dependent from birth and for a very long period thereafter upon other people. He is incapable of developing human personality without a very great deal of accidental or intended help from others.

In the very broadest sense, education is the process which links these three facts together. It is the way the individual acquires the many physical, moral and social capacities demanded of him by the group into which he is born and within which he must function. Sociologists have called this process *socialisation*. Such a term is valuable for two reasons. In the first place, it emphasises that the process is a social one; it takes place in a social context and in ways demanded by the rules of the group. It also allows us to use the word education in a special sense.

Most educators prefer it to mean something in addition to socialisation because, for them discussion of what they are doing usually pre-supposes some ideas about how individuals (and hence society) ought to be improved. For the sociologist there is no difference. Education is the induction of newcomers into a society. It goes on in response to values about how members should act and ideas about what they should learn. These two aspects of 'humanness' —patterns of behaviour and the values which give them 'meaning'—are the two principal foci of sociology.

We now have a broad definition of education. It is all that goes on in society which involves teaching and learning. We can see that this teaching or learning can be either intended or unintended. That is, we need not restrict ourselves only to those consequences of action which are intended. Indeed, to do so would limit our understanding of the educational process unnecessarily. Often the most important consequences of a person's actions are not the ones he was setting out to achieve but the ones which he had not expected. Not only may the consequences be unexpected, they may not even be recognised when they have occurred. Consequently, a basic rule in sociological analysis specifies that in order to understand what education is doing in a particular society, an observer must always distinguish between what educators say it is doing and what it is actually doing. It might happen that these turn out to be similar but there is no reason for him to assume that they are. This idea will be developed later under the headings of *latent* and *manifest* functions.

For most of man's history and for many people today, the process of education simply 'goes on' as a consequence of the functioning of the society or social group into which the child is born. Some effort may be made by adults and older children to teach those laws and customs regarded as vital for the group but little explicit provision is made. Modern society, on the other hand, has set aside particular individuals with a special task to which they can devote the major part of their working energy. The establishment of an occupational category, teacher, involves society in a cluster of rules and ideas about the teaching *rôle*. It also usually requires special arrangements like the allocation of buildings within which the teachers can organise their influencing of children.

Formal and informal education

We are led, therefore, to a major pair of categories accord-

9

ing to which we can divide our analysis of education. It takes place both *formally* and *informally*.

As a consequence of his social experience the developing child absorbs a vast amount of 'knowledge' about the world and how it operates. He will also develop values about how he should interact with it. Informal education is all the teaching and learning which human beings do or undergo during their life-time. An anthropologist described the process in the following way:

> Taking education in its widest sense, we can see readily that it is a process which lasts throughout life. Every new status which an individual acquires, every new condition of life, such as marriage, parenthood, maturity, and old age have to be learned, in that the individual has to adjust gradually and by the acquisition of new attitudes, new ideas, and also new social duties and responsibilities. (Malinowski 1947, p. 141).

Almost all societies have some formalised aspects to their induction of infant or adult newcomers. For example, many preliterate societies will have secret societies or *rites de passage*, during which the neophyte will be subjected to formal educative practives having a fair degree of persuasiveness. Knocking out, or filing down, of teeth, exposure to cold, eating unsavoury food, scourging with nettles and similar 'aids to memory' often accompany the lessons and appear to impress them with great certainty. However, the lessons are often fairly simple. As society becomes more and more economically productive (and hence occupationally specialised) there is a growing dependence upon deliberately organised means of preparing children for adult life. In advanced industrial societies this has reached a point at which preparation could not possibly be left to parents. The rate of social, economic and industrial change has been so great that each succeeding generation must be 'better educated' in many of the skills which are basic to the successful pursuit of occupations. Clearly, parents cannot spend their own energies in providing the needed education, even if they were equipped to do it, and, on the whole, they cannot be. Modern society's solution is the formal system of education. This can be defined as an officially prescribed pattern of rules and objectives allocating tasks, privileges and responsibilities relating to the achievement of certain goals.

On the basis of these ideas, regularities of behaviour are elicited from some people who spend their working lives within the system. The buildings and the behaviour that goes on in them together with the values and rules on which it is based, can all be summarised under the term, *the institution of education*.

Conclusion

All this has been a necessary preliminary to saying what the sociology of education is. It is an application of sociological knowledge, techniques of thinking and of data-collection in examination of the range of social phenomena termed education. In an introductory book of this sort we can do nothing more than outline the main ways in which education is viewed by the sociologist.

Briefly, sociology deals with the process of education under four broad headings:

1. The educational process as an aspect of social interaction,
2. The school as a social group,
3. The influence of other social institutions upon the institution of education,
4. The functions for society of the institution of education.

In offering this set of headings there is no intention of prescribing neat divisions of the field like the slicing of a cake. They are focal points which are useful in summarising the present state of sociological theorising and research on education and they will each form the basis of one of the following chapters.

2
The social animal:
some preliminary perspectives

Culture

In the previous chapter the institution of education was
defined as the material, the patterns of values and the actions which follow from formal arrangements for preparing the individual with the commitments and capacities
thought to be appropriate for life in society. Consequently,
socialisation is fundamental to the education system. For
example, we can study a large business in the same way
that we can study a school, but there will be a difference
in the place which socialisation will have in the analysis.
Within the industrial organisation, socialisation will occur
as a consequence of its functioning. It will not be a major
aim. On the other hand, it is the *raison d'être* of the school.

All socialisation, therefore, is the setting for study of
an educational system. We must begin an analysis of it
by returning to the three fundamental facts about the potential and eventual person with which we began. Linking
these three facts is a strong emphasis upon the importance

of social experience. The human-building ability of society is often best described by using a concept which looks upon the 'way of life' of society as a whole—a *culture*. The culture of a nation or group is a set of shared *symbols* and definitions together with the patterns of behaviour and the material products which they stimulate the people to produce. There are three aspects to it, therefore, the *normative system*, the action system and the material.

The first two aspects of culture (shared symbols and patterns of behaviour) are stated in a way which emphasises the quality of stability which all societies possess if they are to persist. Because of them we can expect a culture to be patterned rather than a disordered jumble of unconnected items and events. The third aspect (the material) on the other hand, is more concerned with changing the world. Karl Marx took an elementary fact of man's existence—that he must win his survival from the world around him—and elevated it to the level of a theory about the force behind social change. In doing so he pointed to the rôle of culture. It is the group's substitute for the instincts with which other animals are equipped in their fight for survival. Instead of 'evolving' towards a new characteristic specially suited to the environment, man develops a technology to suit the same purpose. We do not reproduce people with longer arms and necks to reach up into the trees. We build ladders and fork-lift trucks. From our present vantage-point in history this appears to be both quicker and more efficient. However, a future Martian earth-archaeologist trying to piece together man's pre-holocaust history might conclude differently.

Culture and personality

Culture is not only something which man makes, it is also

something which makes him. There is a very simple way in which this may be shown to be an obvious truism. It is simply not possible for a child to develop into what we know as a human being if he is not brought up in the company of human beings. How he experiences life (and hence what he learns from it) will be greatly influenced by the ways in which he has been taught to think and to value by the culture into which he has been initiated. Thus, the proposition which is basic to sociology claims that the behaviour of human beings is importantly controlled by their relationships with each other and by their memberships in social groups. This is not a statement of certainty and it does not preclude the possibility that, at any time, an individual can raise himself above the limitations on thinking and valuing which have been imposed upon him by his social experience : it only asserts that he is unlikely to.

Such a view of the human situation can be built by following the life of a single member as he experiences socialisation into the group. As a child develops he constantly adds to his perception of himself those ideas which he learns other people have about him. He learns that he is a 'son', a 'brother', white, weak, clever, Baptist, and so on. During play he will also decide that he is a general, a spaceman and a father but he will be able to distinguish his 'real' designations from his 'play' ones. But what do we mean by his 'real' designations? We mean those descriptions which his adult world has prescribed for him. He identifies himself according to the perceptions of reality present in the heads of those around him. Identification of *self* then influences him by controlling his ideas of what he may do in any situation and what he can expect of life. To be 'in' and 'of' society implies that the individual is at the centre of many social forces which must be accepted and adapted to. The socialisation which he has undergone will have seen to it that he has developed habits of thought, ways of perceiving the world and a self-image which encourages adaptation.

This is not an iron process of determinism. It is an approximation. It is hard to imagine a perfectly socialised person in an advanced society if only because of the great flexibility in its rules and regulations. If we think of them as a pattern to which the individual must fit, we would have to say that it is a very sloppy one to which a large number of individual patterns could fit in a rough and ready fashion. There is a great deal of latitude for change since any particular individual can be appreciably out of line without suffering seriously. He then contributes to social change, firstly because he is already part of society himself and secondly because of what he will do to bring about further change.

This 'over-socialised' (Wrong 1961) view is arrived at by concentrating upon what society does to the individual. But the relationship between the individual and the other members of his group is not a simple one which does nothing more than impose upon his mind designations about what he is in society (boy, son, upper class, etc) His actions also help to modify these descriptions, (strong, stupid, good at controlling other, friendly, etc.) in their minds and hence in his own.

Thus the individual takes a part in the construction of his own self. He will develop a concept of 'self in relation to the world around' which is a product of his interaction with his social environment. The presence of such ideas in the mind of a person helps to produce the situation which we described as one of the basic axioms of sociology—that the behaviour of individuals is importantly determined by their relationships with others. That is, what a person does in a particular situation is greatly dependent upon his ideas about what he is and what is expected of him. Since these ideas will have developed in response to the ways in which other people have treated him in the past, there is a fundamental sense in which we can talk of individual actions being controlled by social relations.

Developing a concept of self is only half of the process. An individual must also learn how to interpret the situations in which that self has to operate. A convenient model for describing the symbolising behind behaviour is elucidated in Parson's discussion of the *action-problem situation*. In each situation a person must impose some sort of interpretation upon the vast number of stimuli he receives so as to decide what they mean and ultimately his appropriate responses. This is *cognition*. How a person cognises a situation will be partly a function of how he has learned to interpret stimuli. So far, then, simply seeing what is there is a cultural act. There are also 'response-channelling definitions' which tell the individual whether what he sees is pleasurable or painful to him and whether it is 'good' or 'bad'. These definitions are called *cathectic* and *evaluative* ideas. Once again, cathexes and evaluations are culturally influenced although there is no need to assume that they are only produced by culture.

In studying any society we see that behind the regular patterning of behaviour there are also patterns of rules and regulations which we can conveniently call the normative order. However, the closeness of behaviour to the normative order is not brought about only in the way suggested above. There is more to it than just teaching the individual a view of what he is, what he should do and what he can expect to be able to do. Control of the individual by the group is achieved in various other ways—all, it must be said, of considerably weaker efficiency than this basic piece of personality-building which social living has carried out, and continues to carry out, upon the individual. The systems of *social control* in society can involve physical, psychological or economic threats and sanctions and are usually sufficient to maintain some sort of stability in society.

The inculcation of the normative order is not as simple a job as it sounds because in any society there is a great deal of variation in behavioural norms. Even more importantly, there is always confusion in the meanings attached to the catch-phrases that often stand in lieu of values. Despite this confusion, we would not wish to doubt the power of values to affect behaviour. They lie at the heart of a culture.

The transmission of culture

Schooling, like socialisation, requires *communication*. Amongst human beings this process is an immensely subtle one which derives its complexity from our ability to symbolise.

> A symbol is any voluntary act, event, or record which through social usage has come to stand for something else. The meanings of symbols are arbitrary. They can stand for objects, events, relationships, or other symbols. (O'Brien et. al. 1964, p. 273).

In using symbols man learned not only how to accommodate himself to his environment but also how to adapt the environment to him. In addition, the symbols made it possible for man to transmit from generation to generation the 'knowledge' gained in interaction with nature.

The most important kind of symbols are those that have acquired standard meanings expressed in words throughout a given society or social group. Language has been defined as 'a structured system of arbitrary vocal symbols by means of which members of a social group interact' (Bram 1955,

p. 2). In one sense, then, the world of man is a symbolic creation of his culture. What a human being sees and feels in the world about him is interpreted to him by his culture. A philosopher has taken this idea to its logical extreme:

No longer in a merely physical universe, man lives in a symbolic universe. Language, myth, art and religion are parts of this universe.... No longer can man confront reality immediately; he cannot see it, as it were, face to face.... He has so enveloped himself in linguistic forms, in artistic images, in mythical symbols or religious rites that he cannot see or know anything except by the interposition of this artificial medium. (Cassirer 1944, p. 25)

Apart from its function as a mediator between man and his 'world', language also extends the possible area of social interaction beyond the possible boundaries set by the ordinary limits of person to person contact. We can respond to the thoughts and feelings of people long dead or on the other side of the world. This access to the whole range of thought and experience of man is likely to contribute to the development of ideas particularly in the scientific sphere, but it has several drawbacks in the eyes of many of our apocalyptic social philosophers:

immersion in verbal (as well as non-verbal) symbolism has largely alienated man from nature ... with the expansion of an urban and industrial way of life, we are being increasingly removed from our primary (natural) physical environment and conditioned to functioning with an entirely man-made secondary world of factory whistles, telephone bells, machine control boards, traffic signals, and condensed verbal messages. We are also becoming used to facing human problems outside their flesh and blood context, but instead in terms of legal, political, economic and psychiatric frames of reference. In a sense, man is not at home today in the once familiar world of ordinary physical events: the immediacy of his existence has been sacrificed to the artificial and the intricacies of the symbolic process. (Bram 1955, p. 8).

Remembering that the intelligence tests which still have a function in the different activities of education are strongly biased in favour of the manipulation of abstract concepts, it is not unreasonable to argue that much of our formal education tends to prepare children for just such a world.

Our view of the function of language is specially important to the present stage of research in education. This concentrates upon the ways in which the structure of language influences thinking skills. We tend to assume that language is a simple set of tools which we use as we think fit. They simply 'do the job'; and where they are not adequate, man simply invents new words or symbols which are better fitted. This is very far from the truth because it assumes that ideas are independent of words—that men have ideas and then use words to express them. This has been shown to be an impossible assumption by several linguistic anthropologists who have argued that, at the very least, language and 'knowledge' influence each other. Some psychologists and anthropologists even go so far as to say that language determines what we see rather than vice versa:

We dissect nature along lines laid down by our native languages. The categories and types that we isolate from the world of phenomena we do not find there because they stare every observer in the face.... We cut nature up, organise it into concepts, and ascribe significance as we do, largely because we are parties to an agreement to organise it in this way—an agreement that holds throughout our speech community and is codified in the patterns of our language.... (Benjamin Lee Whorf, quoted in Bram 1955, p. 24)

This idea is beginning to be put to valuable use in analysis of educational problems. For example, it helps in explaining why differences in family background have important connections with differences in school achievement. But it has been introduced at this stage as part of the model of education in society. The intention has been to emphasise the 'interconnectedness' of all aspects of society. The social psychology of human development relates the patterns of social relationships established by the normative order to the development in individuals of social, physical and cognitive skills. The total of these skills is therefore a product of the demands which social structure (the mutual influencing of institutions) makes upon individuals. One of these institutions has a special place insofar as it is a deliberate effort on the part of society to intervene in this situation by taking steps to develop abilities.

Education in social structure

A section in the previous chapter described how education may be looked upon as one of the institutions in society which comprise its *social structure*. In analysing the social structure we look for the ways in which institutions support and influence each other. Each institution has to adapt itself to the requirements of its own environment. Its patterns of action and value will be appropriate to its social environment and susceptible to the changes that go on in it. It will do this by making demands of its members, that is, integrating them into the 'life' of the institution. The whole business can be summarised by describing it at the two separate levels of analysis.

The Institution of Education

(a) has problems of adaptation to its own environment.

(b) it also has problems of integrating its own personnel. Its social life imposes cognitive, cathectic and evaluative requirements upon its members.

The Child

(a) is a product of experience in the different groups within which he is being socialised.

(b) has to adapt to the demands of the education system.

We can regroup these elements by looking outwards from our foci to their environments: —

(i) the institution has an environment which interacts with it. Administrative, economic, social class, religious, etc., patterns of behaviour and values necessarily influence the aims and methods adopted by its personnel.

(ii) the child is surrounded by a social environment comprising patterns of action and valuing which are theoretically analysable as family, social class, religious, etc., groupings of stimuli.

This has been a repetitious set of variations on an elementary theme but it is one which tends not to be understood in a great deal of educational research. The process of education is an aspect of the functioning of society. To gain an adequate picture of this process, we must look at the full picture of mutual influencing between and within social groupings. A purely individual level of analysis runs the risk of taking too much of the social process for granted. Concentration upon the exhibited abilities of individuals to adapt to education has led researchers to commit a kind of 'scientific solipsism' (Hudson 1966) which has tended to obscure rather than clarify what goes on in school.

Research has tended to present a 'front' of respectability for a whole series of beliefs about what happens and ought to happen in school and about what human nature is really like. In failing to take into account the ways in which the social life of the school is intimately related to the patterns of action and values which surround it, we have tended to reify, if not the actual system, at least the *ideologies* (or belief-systems) which supported it.

The warning can be put quite plainly. If we treat the relationship between family background and education as a simple one in which we describe how the home prepared a child for school, we run the risk of forsaking the stance of objectively by putting ourselves in the blinkers which members of the institution of education inevitably have. At the present time we are likely to explain the inability of a child to perform the school tasks as shortage of personal abilities or 'drive'. Yet the same situation could be equally well described as the inability of the school to meet the developmental needs of the child. No more questions are begged that way.

Until recently the bulk of British research has taken the simple educational-technology point of view. The system of education is taken as given and ways are devised of measuring actual (and by inference, potential) adaptability of individual children to it. Since the sociological research of the mid-fifties there has grown up a widespread agreement upon the descriptive facts of the connections between social experience and adaptability to education. But research at the institutional level has been meagre. We have to rely heavily on massive assumptions about the societal consequences of relationships which are measured at the individual level.

There are several levels of analysis involved in the study of education as a social process. Starting with the 'client' we need to look for what it is in his previous experience which improves his adaptivity to schooling. The next stage seeks for the ways in which the patterns of action and behaviour related to group membership in the outside world interact with those of the system of education through their single overlapping part—the child. Once again this research has not been done. We only have a series of assumptions and inferences tied to analysis of the child as a personality rather than to the child as an aspect of social process. We need to know how previous experience produces the cognitive, cathectic and evaluative equipment of the child and the consequences this has for his ability to earn various labels devised by the system for keeping control of the social process going on within it.

The second level of analysis studies how interaction in the school generates 'standards' or criteria for judging social (including academic) behaviour—how it produces the various labels. Study of social process in the school, then, investigates the kind, amount and consequences of social interaction in the school, the genesis of formal and informal rules and the standardisation of behaviour which results.

Finally, the professional teacher and the educational administrator will hold views of what they are, what they can do and what they ought to try to do which are derived from ideologies in the wider society as well as the experiences in the school system. At the same time society actively tries to influence the patterns of interaction in the school through socialisation of teachers, by administrative intervention and through 'public opinion' pressure at national or community level.

Conclusion: Education is the creation of talent

Whatever the gross and obvious contributions of formal education to social change, there is a subtle connection between social change and the collective level of national ability. The previous sections have introduced a view of education in society which is designed to clarify the means by which this relationship operates. Clearly it would be a great mistake to assume that the educational system is the only, or even the major, way in which the total of ability in society is improved. Demands made upon people in the family, and at work, are also vital. The education system is only one setting for the development of self-concept, valued aims, achievement motivation and cognitive skills.

Until the Second World War the thinking of many British educators was dominated by a concept of education which saw it as an exclusive prize to be enjoyed by a few. Hand in hand with this philosophy went a set of beliefs about intellectual capacity, and its distribution, which assumed that potential high ability was strictly limited in any given society. These two beliefs formed a fairly satisfactory (i.e. societally functional) perception of reality as they reinforced each other through the mechanism of self-fulfilling prophecy. That is, a system based upon belief in the existence of a strictly limited supply of high talent which devises special educational arrangements with this in mind, will tend to find evidence supporting such a belief in the consequences of its decisions about clients. There is inevitably a circular process of mutual support. We treat children in ways which assume that they are of a lower standard than others and constantly receive valid evidence to show that they *are* educationally inferior. The tendency we all have towards perceiving what we expect to see, helps teachers to contribute to the strength of the prophecy. But the influence it has upon the self-concepts of children is the vital component in the mechanism.

We can summarise the idea most crudely and in a situation further away from home by a generalisation about the history of the American negro. Until recently the United States treated the negro (as a group) as if he were only fit to be a bootblack. It was then possible to justify this treatment by pointing out that he behaved like one.

Of course, this self-fulfilling prophecy,
evaluation → selective perception of behaviour → evidence → evaluation etc.,

is not an iron process of one hundred per cent certainty. Otherwise, there would never be social change. For many reason, including the inefficiency of many of the human processes we have mentioned and the possibility of crucial experience for individuals, this is only a tendency in society.

One reason why it is difficult to break the prophecy in the position of the negro lies in the presence of an irrelevant but easily identifiable clue, that of skin colour. In the educational world the clues are much more variable and less measurable. Consequently, the process is more haphazard and the possibilities of change far greater.

In Britain, the belief-system of which the two aspects of the prophecy (narrowly limited supply of talent and an educational system geared to finding and dealing with it) form the core, has been giving way in recent years to incorporate a very much greater concern for the socio-cultural context of learning and less restrictive assumptions about potential intellectual capacity.

This appears to have taken place for several reasons. Firstly, since the mid-fifties the demand of industrial societies for high abilities in vast quantities has become a reality in the minds of people concerned with education. Previously the conventional wisdom relating to ability did not counter the perceptions of societal ability-needs too strongly. There was correspondingly less pressure to review the conventional wisdom. Now the pressure is immense and the ideology must be revised.

Secondly, regardless of the fact that *psychometry* has been linked in its assumptions about human nature to *Platonic elitism*, it has been scientific in its intentions. Despite the many opportunities for self- and other-deception in the behavioural sciences, (Thompson 1962) so much good work had to produce some knowledge, and development has occurred. Most importantly, a greater understanding of the assumptions upon which the tests are based and greater conceptual clarity in discussion have developed (Clarke 1962). At the same time research into learning has begun to take much more account of social context.

Thirdly, and perhaps most importantly, the development of anthropology and sociology has focussed attention upon the social nature of man while producing a great deal more knowledge of social and cultural differences.

The final collapse in academic circles of the idea that there is a limited 'pool of ability' in any given society is characterised by the evidence which one of Britain's leading educational psychologists submitted to the Robbins Committee. Dealing with this idea insofar as it has a bearing upon the proportion of the population which can be expected to be able to cope with university work, he insisted that

this reasoning is unsound, and (that) no calculations of the numbers of eligible students can be based on tests of intelligence or other aptitudes, though they could conceivably be based on tests or surveys of aspirations,

27

interests and social attitudes in the population. (Vernon 1963, p. 46)

Professor Vernon's comment typifies the change that has taken place over the last decade in thinking about the distribution and origins of talent in society. From a preoccupation with genetically based 'ceilings' of ability, we are turning to a concern for talent as a consequence of social experience.

A European conference on talent in industrial society followed a similar line in which:

... the most striking agreement that was arrived at in the discussion was the ready abandonment of the metaphor of the 'pool of ability' as scientifically misleading, and from the point of view of policy, irrelevant. The discussion ... moved towards more elaborate social and psychological conceptions of complex processes through which potential qualities are transformed into recognised and educated performances of many different kinds. (Halsey 1961, p. 23)

This culminates in a conviction that the sociological perspective on talent—'... a process of economic and social development is a process of creating ability"—is the one which most reasonably should be acted upon in planning for increased economic efficiency by raising the level of education throughout a nation. The change has been from pessimistic expectations about individual and collective improvement in talent towards optimistic ones.

3
The school

From Gemeinschaft to Gesellschaft

Every kind of culture can be characterised by its fundamental form of social organisation. Folk culture is based
upon *kinship* and mediaeval society depends upon *feudal-
ism* as its method for organising social relationships between its members. With the rise of cities and commerce
a different kind of system became necessary. *Bureaucracy*
is the term often applied to this form. This is not to say
that bureaucracy did not exist before modern times but
that the kinds of social relationships required by bureaucracy have become more essential to the maintenance of
society.

The fairly obvious historical trend which the notion of
increasing bureaucracy attempts to describe has also been
characterised in slightly different ways but always with the
same theme. Maine, for example, perceived the historical
trend as a movement from relationships mostly based upon
status (or position in society) to a great preponderance of

those based upon contract. A major thesis of his work holds that as society developed, so the autonomy of the individual increased. The resultant weakening in social cohesion was made up by an increase in relationships based not upon kinship or fealty but upon contracts.

The change is characterised by increasing importance of specialisation and of rationality applied to the organisation of social life by members of society. It comes about through differentiation in the functions of major institutions and the consequent growth of associations aimed at furthering specific interests. Concomitantly, there has been a trend towards secularism and pragmatism. The value of ways of doing things tends to be measured in terms of their effectiveness in achieving some practical end. Talcott Parsons summarised the trend in the notion that, increasingly, the *dominant value theme* in advanced society is mastery of the world around.

Ferdinand Tönnies described the movement as having taken place from a communal to an associational society, from *gemeinschaft* to *gesellschaft*. In the gemeinschaft type of community a sense of belonging to a group is paramount in that it is an unquestioned fact of life for the individual. Together with this sense of belonging there goes an acceptance of the fundamental perceptual and normative givens of the community. It is above all the community with answers. It determines the individual's perceptions of possible questions and it answers them in terms which seldom leave room for doubt. The individual is born into the gemeinschaft community and his rôles are natural outcomes of his position as a member.

As a contrast, Tönnies described the associational, or gesellschaft, society in which the major social bonds are entered into voluntarily by people engaged in the rational pursuit of their own interests. Such a situation, according to Tönnies, produces the mass society of rootless individuals bound together, not by unquestioned perceptions of reality and an undisputed normative order, but by personal choice. The bond is still there, but it is a much less secure one. It is dependent upon fads and fashions of individual choice and is more prone to rapid change. Because of the decline in the power of norms to control behaviour society develops official rules about behaviour and designates members whose job it is to enforce them.

Bureaucracy

In several ways, therefore, observers have noticed the growing importance of rational and legal restrictions on behaviour which they expected to have serious consequences for individual personalities. They obviously believed that social structure was 'educative' in the sense that it can change personalities. Max Weber pointed to the rational-legal characteristics of the modern organisation as the major contributor to this trend. In doing so he bequeathed us a description of an *ideal-type* or perfect refinement of a rational social organisation.

The expected consequences for personality of his model have earned the almost universal condemnation of social critics and laymen alike and for this reason alone it is worth making the following generalisations. Without bureaucracies our society could not exist and any criticism of them will have to be about how they can be improved. Social panaceas based on a return to the family, to community, to religion or to one of the earlier forms of social organisation are only feasible for protected minorities. Whatever we think about it we cannot maintain our society without deliberately planning social structures. Not the least important of these are the structures devised to inculcate commitments and capacities for adult life in society.

We can expect that as bureaucracies become more important in society the system of education will adopt similar characteristics. If, as educators, we take the view that they are bad for people we have to think how to do something about it. We then have a paradox to face. The system of education is to be one of our important tools but if it is to be effective it will have to become more bureaucratic itself. We will be trying to cure a social illness with a medicine that gets more and more like the poison we are fighting. In such a situation the need to be able to understand the functioning school system as a deliberately constructed social mechanism becomes paramount.

Our first step will be to deal with the concept of bureaucracy as distilled out in Max Weber's ideal type. Fundamentally, a bureaucracy is a rational arrangement of 'offices' providing certain means for administration and control of the office-holders' actions. Officials enter the bureaucracy expecting security, specialisation, salary and seniority based upon achievement and examinations. The rights, duties and qualifications of the official will be carefully defined so that he is replaceable with a minimum of upheaval to the smooth running of the organisation. Offices will be hierarchically arranged so as to facilitate demarcation of responsibility and promotion according to ability. Amongst the intended consequences of all these arrangements are the two attributes which social commentators tend to fear —impersonality and uniformity. If the goals of the organisation are to be achieved the actions of each office holder will have to be predictable according to the specifications of rights and duties attached to his position. The whole arrangement is specifically designed to minimise the personal idiosyncracies and irrationality of the officials. As Weber described it, it is 'dehumanised'.

Perhaps the description has gone far enough to raise serious doubts about its relevance to education. It can fit either a school or a national system only in certain superficial ways. Nevertheless, if we have to find a single term to describe the likely development of education in the future, it will probably be increased bureaucratisation. Apart from this the school will be principally engaged in fitting children for life in what are known as bureaucracies. Finally, as we shall see, the study of formal organisation is still in its infancy and rapidly moving away from the need to employ the Weberian ideal-type as a yard-stick.

Etzioni's classification of organisations

In the hope of strengthening this movement Etzioni (1964) has suggested that the term bureaucracy should be replaced by the non-emotive 'organisation'. His view is that Weber's ideal-type, in its concentration upon the rational-legal aspects of a large organisation diverts our attention from the equally important non-rational exercise and *legitimation of authority*. Gouldner (1954) developed this distinction into a theory that there are two types of bureaucracy—representative and punishment-centred. The first contains authority based upon knowledge and expertise. Its rules are agreed upon by the participants who justify them as the most suitable means to the desired ends. Coercion to obey the rules, therefore, must take the form of persuasion, education or non-violent brainwashing.

The *punishment-centred* bureaucracy, on the other hand, contains authority which depends upon office holding. Rules in this case are imposed in accordance with the status hierarchy and enforced by punishment of a more explicit or formal kind.

If we try to apply either of these two concepts to a school or a school system we will clearly find ourselves leaving out a great deal that matters. Authority in the school and in the school system derives from either or both sources, depending upon the situation. The pupil-teacher relationship in many schools fits the punishment-centred type. On the other hand, the notion of representative authority is a powerful justification for rule-making by teachers for pupils and by head teachers for teachers. Having constructed a set of concepts in our heads we have still to do the more difficult job of applying them usefully to actual situations.

Etzioni (1961) grapples with the problems of variations from the bureaucratic ideal-type by suggesting a nine-fold typology summarising different kinds of compliance. In addition to looking at how our organisation enforces authority we must consider the kind of involvement which it stimulates in the members. The compliance relationship is a two-sided one : —

A TYPOLOGY OF COMPLIANCE RELATIONS

Kinds of Power	Kinds of Involvement		
	Alienative	*Calculative*	*Moral*
Coercive	1	2	3
Remunerative	4	5	6
Normative	7	8	9

In this typology Gouldner's representative bureaucracy becomes normative power and his punishment-centred becomes coercive power. To these Etzioni adds remunerative power.

People 'go along' with the organisation in ways which are either grudging, calculating or morally involved. Etzioni has no doubt that certain pairs of these six categories tend to go together—1, 5 and 9 are all congruent types in which type of compliance follows from kind of power. However, the incongruent types of organisation do exist because the organisation does not have total power over participants and hence compliance relationships in other organisations influence the actions and attitudes of members. Nevertheless, he does believe that congruent types are more effective in achieving their goals. Coercive, utilitarian and normative compliance are not only the more effective forms. They are also the states towards which organisations tend to change.

He goes further than these assumptions for he also believes that the types of congruent compliance relate with the kind of goal for which the organisation was formed. There are three broad kinds of goal: —

A TYPOLOGY OF GOALS AND COMPLIANCE

Type of Compliance	Organisational Goal		
	Order	*Economic*	*Culture*
Coercive	1	2	3
Utilitarian	4	5	6
Normative	7	8	9

Once again the diagonal represents congruent types towards one of which the organisation would tend to change.

All this involves some interesting, if yet untested, hypotheses which would have great value in educational analysis. For example, we would expect that a school requires normative compliance for cultural goals. What happens in a school in which the major goal is order? Presumably, the type of compliance would tend to be coercive, but this presupposes a likelihood of alienative involvement on the part of participants—you might have order in the establishment but a rejection of it when the participant is free.

However, it is difficult to avoid the feeling that this very neat set of types harbours a whole series of psychological assumptions which are an integral part of the democratic ideology but which may be empirically incorrect. There seems, for example, to be as much valid educational evidence in support of a relationship between coercive power and moral involvement (number 3) as there is evidence supporting an association between coercive power and alienative involvement (number 1). The Hitler youth movement, Jewish theological, classical Chinese and Spartan education give very little support to Etzioni's hypothesis. Indeed one of the unsolved mysteries of education (unsolved perhaps to all but Freudians) is the power which genuinely coercive educational regimes have of inculcating moral commitment and attaining cultural goals.

Perhaps Etzioni's hypotheses look so convincing not only because they coincide with democratic values but also because in a democratic environment they will tend to work. It is fairly likely that an ordinary secondary school (not selective because this exaggerates the calculative-economic element) attempting to operate through coercive power would produce alienative involvement. It could be that this is because it is impossible for it to be properly coercive. It is not the coerciveness but the gap between the manifest desire of those in authority to be coercive and their equally obvious failure to achieve it that produces the alienative compliance.

Whatever the objective truth of these relationships Etzioni's arrangement of concepts improves our ability to discuss the process of education. As a start we might agree with him that bureaucracy is an unnecessary term which should be replaced by 'organisation', defined as a social unit characterised by :

(1) division of labour, power, and communication responsibilities, divisions which are not random or traditionally patterned, but deliberately planned to enhance the realisation of specific goals;

(2) the presence of one or more power centres which control the concerted efforts of the organisation and direct them towards its goals; these power centres must also review continuously the organisation's performance and re-pattern its structure, where necessary, to increase its efficiency;

(3) substitution of personnel, i.e. unsatisfactory people can be removed and others assigned their tasks. The organisation can also recombine its personnel through transfer and training. (Etzioni 1964, p. 3)

When we employ this sort of a perspective in looking at education we are dealing with the school itself. Perhaps by a stretch of the imagination we can see the whole structure of organised education in Britain as a single organisation with the Minister of Education as the head, the Local Education Authorities as sections and the schools as individual factories or units, but it is probably stretching the concept too far. This is not because one cannot conceive of so vast an organisation but because there are many aspects of the system of education which lead one to suspect that the term 'institution' is more valuable. If there is a range of variation in the extent to which organisations approach Etzioni's definition we must expect that schools in Britain will tend to come farther away from it than an army or an industrial enterprise.

Under his first characteristic the divisions of labour (who

does what?) are to some extent deliberately planned to achieve specific ends but there is also a very strong element of traditionalism in the decisions made about the jobs to be done by teachers and by children. The young arts graduate, still working hard on his T. S. Eliot image is often rudely shocked to find that he is automatically deemed to be the choice for football team coaching according to the long-standing school tradition that the youngest member of staff is always fittest to undergo the rigours of watching football. Similarly, the curriculum content, a major justification for the existence of the school, will be dependent upon a very powerful tradition about proper knowledge and activities.

The second characteristic is met, more or less, in the school where the headteacher is a source of power who operates to increase the efficiency of the organisation. He is not likely to cut as dashing a figure in this respect as the managing director of a factory producing hair-clips because of the differences in establishing criteria for efficiency. But the headteacher does have a certain degree of authority over his staff and pupils. Perhaps more importantly, he also has an opportunity to develop leadership relations with them. Together, authority and leadership make it feasible for the headteacher to direct the actions of his staff in ways he expects to achieve the goals of the school as he sees them. However, the school is in a difficult position compared with an enterprise of private industry. It does not have a standardised universal token like money by which all events can be evaluated and it is therefore subject to pressure towards measuring achievement of goals by specifying them in certain practical ways—a school is doing well if its 11 + or A level rate goes up.

As a general rule, the third characteristic is met even less well. The traditional security of tenure and the very high degree of academic autonomy which the teacher enjoys reduce the extent to which the secondary school, in particular, can meet it. As we will see later, professionalism is often a barrier to the achievement of a rational form of organisation.

Bidwell's analysis of American education

The most perceptive use of organisational concepts has been made by Bidwell (1965) who suggested that there were four major organisational attributes of the North American school system. Two are characteristics of its personnel: the arrangements of pupils into 'age-grade cohorts' and the contractual hiring of its staff members as trained and licensed professionals. The third is its special combination of bureaucracy and structural looseness. Finally, he saw that the dual responsibility of its officers— to a clientele and to a public constituency—imposes a series of prescriptions and proscriptions upon the actions of teachers.

One of the problems involved in devising an organisational framework for analysis of the school system lies in the ambiguous position of the pupils. Are they members of it or are they the clients it serves? If it is the latter what do we mean by serve? Bidwell begins his analysis with the proposition that schools are client-serving institutions. If this were to mean that the pupils should be thought of as the clients—as something distinct from the organisation— we would be removing vital aspects of both its formal and informal structuring. He takes this into account by distinguishing between student and staff rôles within the organisation. The student rôle is a recruitment one and compulsory. On the other hand, the staff achieve and hold their positions in the light of professional qualifications.

There is therefore a fundamental distinction between the rights and responsibilities of the two types of personnel, which influences how they view each other and consequently how they interact. In crude terms, when a pupil asks 'why do we have to do this?' the answer is some variant of 'because I say you ought to.' When a teacher asks the same question the answer will either be 'because you are paid to' or 'because it is an ethical requirement of the profession which you have chosen to join.' Disagreement between students and staff over this dichotomy is one aspect of the present student unrest throughout the world.

The third characteristic of the system Bidwell calls its distinctive combination of bureaucracy and structural looseness. All American and British school systems are bureaucratic to some extent. For example, the staff are office-holders who are recruited according to criteria of merit and competence. Their position is secure under contract and the requirements of their work are laid down with some specificity. There is some division of labour between them and a fairly clear hierarchy of authority. Administrative work goes on according to rules of procedure which set limits to the discretionary powers of officers by specifying both the aims and the modes of official action. However, it would be unwise to carry this rational view of the structure of the school or even an educational system very far, for such limitations on teaching behaviour are fragmentary. Certainly the rudiments of bureaucracy are there, but one important characteristic of the teacher rôles transcends the individual requirements of a single system. This is his professionalism.

But professionalism plays a dual part in industrial undertakings. Most importantly it offers an alternative to a centralised authority structure. At the same time it causes structural complexities that produce communication problems and require the assistance of centralised administrative apparatus. Two separate kinds of staff structures result—the large managerial staff in the central offices and the professionals who tend to concentrate in the schools. How this matters for the functioning of the system is a problem for research but it seems to be reasonable to expect that it will.

Professionalism is an important way of dealing with the organisational needs for division of labour and for an authority hierarchy, but it is a non-bureaucratic way. A professional is asumed to have both the appropriate value-commitments and the technical skills for doing the job. There is theoretically no need to devise specifications about how each task is to be carried out because the professional will know. Of course, in real life professionals do not work together in quite that way. On the surface the professional ethic must be preserved and to criticise or report on the professional activities of a 'colleage' is un-professional The administrative absurdity of this situation is modified both formally and informally. At the formal level the administrative structure imposes restrictions upon what teachers may do. Informally, colleagues attempt to control each other's behaviour through the powerful social mechanisms of 'co-operation', opprobrium and gossip.

Professional restrictions, however, are effective only in extreme and obvious circumstances—a teacher can be dismissed for sexual assault but never for psychological assault. Usually they are ineffective—a teacher who is psychologically able to ignore the advice, pleas, ridicule and gossip of colleagues has an unparalleled degree of latitude for personal decision-making in the classroom.

It is probably most useful to look upon the school as an existing social group which has to adapt itself to internal and external demands, some social interactional and some formal, or administrative. The distinction between these two kinds of demands will be difficult to draw particularly when the demand matters to how the school functions. It will be simple, that is, to identify a formal administrative rule specifying the body responsible for the maintenance of school window-sills and occasionally use may be made of aspects of this administrative environment of the school to force actions upon it. But in general, such questions do not seriously influence the social process in the school. On the other hand, an Inspector of Schools or subject organiser can have a great influence on a school but it would be difficult to describe it as administrative rather than social interactional influence.

Bidwell describes a fourth characteristic of the American school system as the dual responsibility of its officers to a clientele and to a public constituency. This is probably a much less important characteristic in Britain than in America and better treated as an aspect of professionalisation. It is not that British teachers are irresponsible but only that one aspect of professionalism—control within the profession of judgements about the consequences of its work —is much more powerful in Britain. Most importantly, there is very little sense of responsibility to a public constituency other than either the school itself or society. Even responsibility to the client—either parent or pupil—tends to be specified according to the rules made by the profession. To exaggerate only slightly, if a parent wishes to criticise a teacher he must do so according to the professional's definitions of the desired consequences of education and the legitimacy of the means to be employed for achieving them, rather than according to his own definitions.

In Britain, therefore, even more than in the United

States, we can argue that the education system is best described as one of social groups (schools) linked by administrative procedures and professional ideologies.

The object has been to emphasise the danger in assuming that a conventional organisational analysis as developed in American business enterprises can offer anything more than helpful insights into the functioning of the British school system at the present time. However, as Dubin (1959) has pointed out there are several ways in which the organisation can be treated. Amongst sociologists and political scientists bureaucracy as an administrative type has been the central focus. From this point of view we have concluded that such administration as goes on in the system is devoted to maximising the opportunities of professionals (rather than office holders) to make professional decisions (rather than decisions based on organisational requirements). The decisions are made in working towards vaguely defined and often contradictory goals which are judged on objective-seeming criteria like examination performance. So far it has been argued that if we employ the administrative type of bureaucracy as a means for analysing education we will have to give greatest weight to the ways in which professionals protect their independence of action from their clients, other professionals and administrators.

Dubin identified four other kinds of analysis which offer complementary strategies for arriving at useful insights into the functioning educational system. Briefly, they concentrate on the conflict between the individual psyche and its organisational restrictions, the organisation as patterns of interaction, the organisation as a structure of rules and the organisation as patterns of behaviour. All four of these have the advantage which the bureaucratic approach lacks of not prejudging the issue by deciding that the formal administrative structure has the Weberian characteristics and is the crucial means by which changes in the system are brought about. Both of these assumptions are very likely to be incorrect in a given organisation. The final sections of this chapter, therefore, will offer a simplified amalgamation of the other perspectives as a complement to the bureaucratic one.

People-processing social establishment

Brim and Wheeler (1966) suggest that if we are to understand the workings of a school as a formal organisation we must recognise that a special characteristic distinguishes it from other kinds of deliberately constructed organisations —it processes people rather than things. The difference is a vital one because the processing takes place through talking to a product which has the capacity to answer back. The processing organisation itself, therefore, is also a part-product of its product. Finally, the product also talks to other units of production, ahead or behind it in the production line, satisfying its needs or having failed them.

The reverend Dodson must have had the problems of an educational analyst in mind when he described Alice's difficulty in following the croquet game. In the conventional game the equipment is inanimate and can be mastered by practice based on an assumption of standard performance in response to use. But in the dream-croquet equipment was animate. Instead of allowing its head to hit the hedgehog-ball the flamingo would bend its neck in its own kind of response to what it was undergoing, while the hoops would uncurl and walk away. In the same way the human apparatus in the game of education responds to how it is being handled and the goals of the activity are apt to be shifting and indeterminate.

Fortunately, for many of the reasons outlined in earlier chapters social behaviour is not entirely random. The very existence of social structures like schools proves that. But such a statement is hardly worth making. What we need to know is how they are patterned and the factors behind their development.

We must start with the reason for the structure—its goals. It is easy to insist at this point that organisations do not have goals but that people do, thereby reducing the problem to one of individual motivation. To do so would miss the point because while we clever people who write and read books about schools know it, people who live and work in organisations do not (even when they are the same person). What really matters is that people in the organisation believe it to have goals and they adjust their behaviour accordingly.

A primary distinction to be drawn amongst kinds of goals for a socialising organisation is that between rôle socialisation and status socialisation. (Parsons 1959). Do the functionaries and clients of an organisation perceive it to be preparing its output with skills to do particular jobs or with social skills to behave in ways which are appropriate to particular positions in society? To some extent this is an unreal distinction since all skills are susceptible to social context both in the learning and in the performance. Nevertheless, conflict over them in the minds of both or either kind of participant is part of the social life of the establishment. Particularly when the organisation is large, it may very well develop two different staff systems to deal with the two kinds of socialisation goals. One group would work to develop the practical skills like typewriting and carpentry while the other concentrates upon status preparation. In Britain the division of labour is often developed between socialisation units rather than within them. That

45

is, most educators would tend to look upon education as status-socialisation, whereas rôle-socialisation must be reserved for either technical and professional schools or 'on the job' training. Conversely, there would be many teachers in status-socialising establishments who define their goals in rôle-terms and vice-versa. The possibilities for conflict are many. The secondary modern school which causes its pupils to develop an image of it as a social establishment aiming for status-socialisation will find them to be troublesome because they expect rôle-socialisation.

A version of the status versus rôle-socialisation conflict can also be found in assumptions made about the extent to which socialisation is to be in the interests of the client or of society. Once again, the distinction is often a false one but variations in emphasis on one or the other side are found in attitudes held by members of the same establishment. Inevitably the client tends only to have the individual emphasis except insofar as he has been socialised into an identification with the school as a group having goals which are legitimate simply because they belong to it.

The two pairs of emphases are at the bottom of conflict over the goals of socialisation but they do not form the basis of a full explanation for goal-setting behaviour. A crucial factor in the different conflicts will be the extent to which clients participate in goal-setting. This is a complicated question because the product can answer back during processing and thereby change the socialiser's view of what he is aiming for. We tend to assume that the extent to which a client participates in discussion of the goals will vary directly in relation to his ultimate level of acceptance of the final agreements.

The formal structure itself also contributes to the formation of groups within it. For example, the organisation usually imposes ranking designations of some kind usually related to age or achievement. Such a scheme is inevitably reflected in systems of typing or ranking developed by the clients. It will not necessarily be the same as the organisational scheme, but it will take into account and will tend to be much more closely related to the needs and goals of the clients. If the school lays great stress upon academic achievement in its ranking the client system of ranking will take account of the designations used but may rank them in a different way—a 'brilliant mind' or 'A-streamer' is also a 'four-eyed swot'. The designation is the same but the ranking different. Interaction between organisational and client-based typing systems will be a function of the extent to which the former is understood by the clients to be serving their own needs and goals. In turn, their perceptions of their needs and goals will be a function of 'outside' socialisation responding to 'inside' experiences.

Education in a social establishment

A social establishment is any place surrounded by fixed barriers to perception in which a particular kind of activity regularly takes place. I have suggested that any social establishment may be studied profitably from the point of view of impression management. Within the walls of a social establishment we find a team of performers who co-operate to present to an audience a given definition of the situation. This will include the conception of own team and of audience and assumptions concerning the ethos that is to be maintained by rules of politeness and decorum. We often find a division into back region, where the performance of a routine is prepared and front region where the performance is presented. Access to these regions is controlled in order to prevent outsiders from coming into a performance that is not addressed to them. Among members of the team we find that familiarity prevails, solidarity is likely to develop and that secrets that could give the show away are shared and kept. (Goffman 1959, p. 238)

Goffman did not have a school in mind when he wrote the above paragraph but any teacher would recognise its relevance. Particularly, if we think of the school as adult staff and the pupils as its audience, he is describing an important aspect of the educational process. Organising education is fundamentally a question of impression-management. That is, deliberate planning and implementation are attempts to manipulate the impressions in the heads of actors and audience. But this is only the first step in analysis. We have also to look for the unintended effects upon impressions which follow from actions. The crucial reason for this was dealt with in the previous chapter. Social interaction is the means by which the 'concept of self' develops in the individual.

Goffman was suggesting that an individual learns to manipulate this situation by deliberately fabricating the clues which his behaviour offers to people around him. This does not invalidate the self concept picture—it only makes it more complex. An individual's ability to manage impressions is dependent upon the kind of latitude or credibility permitted by his social situation. His own previous history of behaviour and the ways in which it has been evaluated by the group will play an important part in this. In addition, his own view of the situation and of his own position in it will provide him with advice upon what he can achieve. Once again this will be a function of his previous history in this and other groups or situations. His impression-management behaviour will itself be partially controlled by the group. Following Goffman, therefore, we can take the school as an example of a social establishment and describe the process of education as the consequences of deliberate or accidental impression management.

In order to carry out its function of inculcating the commitments and capacities for adult life the institution of education is forced constantly to evaluate the extent to which its clients are reaching the required standards. Unlike in the economy where the standard or number of goods is measured, the product is people. We can use this fact to justify the following description of the school which will help to explain the social processes and their consequences for individuals.

The social process of interpersonal evaluation

There are certain forces acting in any situation where one individual interacts with another. Firstly, A will be judged according to criteria which B has learned in his own social experience. Thus a teacher might be rated highly by her head teacher because of the sobriety of her dress, but be coolly received by her girl pupils because she is dowdy. Or the reverse—a teacher, rejected for appointment in one school because she was too 'dressy' might be a great success in another because the girls feel she takes care of her appearance. In both cases, two different sets of values lead the evaluators (head-teachers and girl-pupils) to contradictory attitudes towards the same individual. The evaluators' attitudes will also influence their judgement on other aspects of the teacher's performance. Secondly, social experience will lead the individual to develop certain standards and values which are reflected in his or her own behaviour —in this case, ways of dressing.

In the act of social evaluation, then, forces come together from two directions: from 'above', the evaluator brings his own standards and values, and from 'below', the evaluee exhibits his. The resulting judgement in the mind of the evaluator will be based, to a large extent, upon a matching up of the values which he infers from clues picked up from the behaviour of the evaluee. For the sake of completeness we also have to note that in a two-person interaction each is *both* evaluator and evaluee. To this we must add the fact that the judgement is not only overtly in the mind of the evaluator, it is also implicit in the way in which he behaves towards the evaluee. It is not simply a question of one person deciding that another is stupid, dangerous, or interesting and then deciding on how he is to be treated. A person can unwittingly treat another in a way which amounts to an evaluation without intending or realising it. Finally, it is not so much how the evaluator intends to treat the evaluee that matters but how the evaluee experiences that treatment.

The whole life of the school is a continuous process of evaluations of this sort. Each pupil and each teacher is constantly, implicitly or deliberately, evaluating each other. These evaluations range from relatively impermanent or transient views to permanent ones which influence all interaction between evaluator and evaluee over long periods of time and which may be communicated to other evaluators. Because the school is formally set up with the explicit intention of making evaluations it also makes a formal attempt to record them. It does this by testing and sorting.

The testing is fairly easily explained. Adult personnel of the school try to distil out their standards relating to achievement in school subjects. These are often misnamed objective tests. It would be much more accurate to look upon them as reifications of the subjective evaluation underlying the life of the school. Admittedly, they are more objective than a teacher's impressions and can act as a kind of check upon them. Nevertheless, if we look at the culture of the school as a whole we realise that such a group generates ideas about physical, social and intellectual behaviour which look like simple descriptions to the members but which are evaluations representing unintentional choice between alternatives. A fish, it is said, would be the last to discover that water was important to it. Applying this idea to schooling the objective tests of school achievement are really tests of certain kinds of social skills involving concentration on memorising and repeating printed symbols. As Hudson (1966) shows, the school in its concern for what it believes to be intellectual ability tends to minimise the importance of creative thinking.

Reification of the evaluating content of social process also occurs through actual sorting decisions. The school organises itself in order to simplify, standardise and universalise the evaluating that has to be done. Definitions of the situation have to be standardised in any social establishment if communication is to be quick and easy. An answer to the question, "what form are you in?", will quickly define the universe of possible action open to the questioner. Inevitably, because this kind of social establishment is devoted to evaluating children on academic criteria it formalises its judgements by officially describing its clients according to 'academic standards' as they are understood in the establishment.

The controversy on 'streaming' is basically one in which presumed organisational consequences are set against presumed personality consequences. Unfortunately, they are presumed rather than known consequences, because the research on both sides of the equation is inadequate. Particularly, there has been no research on the organisational efficiency of streaming. On the other hand the weight of research evidence tends to argue that the consequences of streaming for the self-concept and hence for the 'ability' of the child are deleterious for those designated low and average achievers. On these grounds the Department of Education and Science decided to end the most conclusive kind of streaming in the educational system—that of streaming by schools.

Adaptation to education

Previous sections have put together a model of the school as a social process in which all members are constantly evaluating each other's actions and modifying their behaviour accordingly. Such a model has been chosen because it provides a link between two other models—that of formal structure and that of self-concept development. We are now in a position to put them together so as to provide a picture of the school which recognises that they are just different ways of describing the same thing. The structure of this social establishment is formed by regular patterns of behaviour relating to a normative order of explicit (or formal) and unwritten laws. These, in turn, contain the assumptions about what is good in both the moral and the efficiency sense. Members of the social establishment inevitably find themselves playing the games of social interaction on terms which have developed in it. This is true even when they are dissatisfied with their own treatment.

For example, Lacey (1966) describes how streaming in a grammar school encouraged the development of an 'anti-group' whose members rejected what the school stood for and refused to do what was expected of them. Most significantly, in trying to leave school the boys had accepted the school's evaluation of them as students who couldn't cope with the work. The absurdity of the implicit assumption in school and child that a pupil judged at 11 years to be in the top 20% of all human intellects could not have understood Pythagoras' Theorem or Boyle's Law or learned French often escapes both parties to the mutual deception.

No distinction has been made between formal and informal rules or between standards of moral goodness as opposed to efficiency because from the point of view of this model the distinctions are arbitrary. The formal-informal dichotomy, particularly, can be most misleading in analysis of schools because it distorts the picture of how the establishment functions by encouraging the belief that rules are made by teachers and administrators. This is only half the truth and the easy half to see. Much more importantly we must be able to recognise the extent to which actions of adult staff are controlled by group processes. There is a real sense in which a teacher who does not understand the forces of social interaction influencing his behaviour in the classroom is a puppet. He makes decisions which he believes to be his own and perceives social situations which he believes to be objectively there, but all are a function of the group processes in which he is enmeshed.

Similarly, distinctions between social and intellectual behaviour are usually false. Within the school system ideas about intellectual behaviour must be understood as a function of the social process. Exhibited thinking skills cannot be understood apart from the social context, and explanations of how they have developed must normally look to previous experience.

Explicit and implicit evaluation, a permanent aspect of all interaction, is an underlying process which supports the more obvious structure of decisions about teachers and pupils. As we will see in Chapter V the outcome of this process is related to the sytem of *stratification* in the wider society. Swift (1965a) for example found that the children of middle class parents had six times as good a chance of selection at 11 + as working class children. The simple class-chances figures could not be explained by deliberate social class prejudice on the part of the educational decision-makers. They do not say that one group of individuals shall be failed because they belong to a particular *social class* and that others shall be passed because they belong to a different one. We have to look for the mechanisms by which the social evaluations are included in the 'objective' evaluations like arithmetic, English and intelligence tests. We can expect that this will occur in three basic ways.

Firstly, from above. The tests will test those skills which the school personnel consider to be good. What they consider to be good will depend upon what they have learned at least partly in a social class situation. Intelligence tests will often include items which contain social class-linked knowledge, motivations, thinking skills and speaking skills. Secondly, from below. The child brings to the situation the habits of thought, social knowledge and motivations which he has learned within a social class sub-culture. Thirdly, the interaction between the two sets of forces has important consequences for the actual performance level of the child by affecting, over the years, the development of this self-concept of ability, his motivation to achieve and hence his level of ability. It also matters for the developement of the teacher's self concept of ability and perception of reality.

The social establishment provides an environment within which there operates a cycle of mutual influencing between each personality and its environing social process. An individual's personality is both an aspect of this social process and a separate entity responding to it. If we follow the experience of a single pupil we can see how the total social process is a summation of individual accommodations. It is possible to distinguish conceptually between two levels at which cultural experience will affect the accommodation of an individual to the demands of an institution. Firstly, the process of accommodation involves a clash between the cognitive, cathectic and evaluative skills which are demanded or implicitly expected in the school. This culture clash logically varies from virtually none to extreme. Both ends of the clash occur in Britain today. At one end we will find perhaps the vicar's son at a parish school whose teacher looks upon the vicar's family as a model of Christian behaviour. At the opposite end we have a seven-year-old Pakistani child entering a Bradford school in the first week of his arrival in Britain.

The two levels at which this culture clash occurs we can call the direct and latent levels. The direct level refers to the situation in which motivations to attain the goals of a social group are not adequate in comparison with the norms of goal motivation which are present in the group. This is the level at which explanation for lack of success in the educational system usually starts. A working class boy leaves the grammar school early because he wants to earn 'good money' as second man on a demolition lorry. He does not accept the school value that education is all important. There is a simple conflict between the value the school requires him to hold about going to school and the one he actually holds.

Cultural clash at the latent level occurs when the cognitive, cathectic and evaluative requirements of the social group within which the individual was socialised are not consonant with those of the school group into which he is moving. To the extent that this clash occurs, adaptation of the individual to the new situation is obstructed. This can happen regardless of the desire to adapt on the part

55

E

of the individual concerned. The working class boy with good intentions and parental backing who 'just hasn't got it' is a common enough phenomenon in the grammar school. The boy wants to do well, does as he is told, causes no real trouble, but just does not do very well. Inevitably the teachers tend to explain this as lack of brain power— but cultural clash at the latent level might often be a better explanation. He does not properly understand what is going on and fails to respond to the underlying requirements of school life. His perceptions of what school is, of what 'achieving well' is, his conception of the environment, of his own abilities and of what teachers are taking for granted, may all conspire against his successful adaptation regardless of his desire to do well.

The clash is not a single experience like an examination. It is a series of experiences stretching over the years each of which has some effect upon the individual's own picture of what he is and what he can expect to be able to do. We have not done enough, therefore, in showing that there can be a clash. We have to consider how that clash contributes to the self-concept of the pupil, because we know that people are likely to do those sorts of things that (a) they think other people expect of them and (b) that they expect themselves to be able to do. Both of these sets of ideas are learned in social situations, and it is by this means that the school influences the development of the child. It provides the experience which contributes to the growth of his or her self-concept.

Conclusion—The process of education

This chapter has brought together many different perspectives and findings of behavioural science. Its object has been to provide a picture of the educational system in motion.

At present, and until the system takes on many more of the characteristics of modern large-scale organisations, the emphasis has been upon the school as a social establishment with a culture of its own. Each school has adaptation problems in the face of its own environment which are solved in ways which have consequences for its personnel and clients.

The one special characteristic of such a social establishment (as opposed to other kinds like a factory or a community) is that it is specifically required to pay attention to its own normative and behavioural system. That is, if we think of pupils as part of the establishment rather than its clients, what in other establishments would be the means for achieving ends are actually the ends. Put rather too simply the school is a group of people with standards which it is the job of the paid personnel to maintain. Other institutions maintain their standards in order to achieve something else. Schools, in maintaining their standards, are actually achieving what they are there for because their members are their product.

It has been shown that standards are to an important extent a function of group processes forged in interaction and tempered by experience of it. Because experience of these standards has a fundamental influence upon ability in a whole range of behaviours—intellectual, social and physical—there is a built-in tendency towards stability. Individuals are constantly receiving evidence in the behaviour of others that their view of them is correct.

Two levels of evaluation or typing (that is the application of standards to one another) was defined. On the surface the school officially ties labels upon pupils and staff. Members are prefects, A-streamers, bottom of the form, senior masters, lower-school and so on. But this structure of formal typing is rather like the tips of a mountain range showing through a heavy cloud and seen from above. Beneath them lies the supporting topographical detail. In the same way the sub-stratum of evaluation implicit in all social interaction supports its peaks of formal typing. The stresses and strains present in the mountain range determine its shape, with modifications caused by external factors like climate and the activities of men. Similarly, the official contours of social typing are a function of the underlying stresses of social interaction.

The official typing patterns are guides to the sub-stratum evaluation but many other factors intervene to make the relationships far from rigid. People misunderstand each other, individuals refuse to conform and people change. Consequently, the patterns are also subject to what goes on below them. Most importantly they are susceptible to the changing ways of thinking and perceptions of reality in the outside world because the ideology of teaching is an aspect of wider politico-religious ideologies.

The picture we must keep in our minds of the school, therefore, is of a living organism to which individuals must adapt while coping with environmental pressures. In the process it is receptive to change from within and without. Stability is maintained through standards and their influence upon personality, but it is a kind of mobile stability which makes it a part of changing society as well as a contributor to the change.

4

The social environment of the institution of education

The socio-cultural environment

Two aspects of social environment are important in the study of education—that of the child and that of the system. This is not to say, of course, that there are two environments, but only that there are two important perspectives from which the social process may be viewed. In both cases the environment consists of intersecting and overlapping social groups and institutions.

In looking at the school as a social establishment surrounded by other groups we have to discover the extent to which it is able to control its own life. Conversely, how far and in what ways is it susceptible to influences from other groups? There are some very obvious ways in which outside groups can influence the functioning of the school. For example, a school in a community which is dominated by a single powerful industry may be forced by the sheer necessity of its responsibility for the career opportunities of its pupils to organise itself in ways which suit the needs of that industry. There is, however, a much more complicated level at which the influencing takes place. In this case we have to look at the extent to which the value-system and behaviour patterns of 'outside' groups interpenetrate those held by the personnel of the school. A simple diagram illustrates the inter-relations between the four elements.

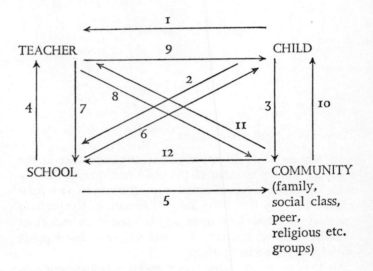

Relationships:

1, 2, 3. The child brings his own intellective skills and habits, attitudes, values, perceptions of reality to teacher, school and community.

4, 5, 6. The school is a social organisation with its behavioural and value requirements to which child and teacher adapt. It will also have an unavoidable influence upon the surrounding community : it influences attitudes and knowledge of the community particularly in relation to education; its manpower output influences social structure.

7, 8, 9. The teacher brings intellective skills and habits, attitudes, values and perceptions of reality to interact with those of the child, school and community.

10, 11, 12. Community influences the formal organisation of the school (governors, P.T.A., administration, politics etc.). It makes demands upon the teacher, 'produces' the child before school and interacts with it through the child.

The diagram is only a simple characterisation of the social process from which the four elements are abstractions. Nevertheless, incomplete as the descriptions are, they do call attention to the reciprocal ways in which each element influences each of the others. The present chapter will deal with the groups which comprise the 'community'.

The major groups are formed by *families*, *social classes*, *peer groups* and *religions*. Its administrative setting comprises the formal structures set up to administer the school. In certain cases it is also reasonable to look upon the area surrounding a school as a total community. It has a particular geographical, economic and historical setting which may very well have encouraged its inhabitants into unique ways of doing things and of valuing what they do. Locality, then, can also be a factor affecting what goes on in a school. To put the idea properly; the concept of local *community* may be a useful device for analysing the relationships between a school and its environment. Finally, all the people surrounding the school form its population or *demographic* environment.

The demographic environment

The manpower problems of education are of two kinds—institutional and societal. By this we mean that the system has its own problems of manpower input and responsibility to society for its output. In this section we have to look at the population structure as an environment for the educational system because it can have great importance for what is done, or attempted, in schools. All the important variables are mentioned in the following extract:

During the last ten years when the number of pupils in maintained schools in England and Wales has risen by nearly 700,000 or about 11 per cent, the number of teachers has risen by about a quarter, so that the pupil/ teacher ratios have improved and the size of classes has been reduced. There is still a considerable way to go, however, before all classes can be reduced to the prescribed limits. In the next few years the school population will rise much more rapidly, because of the rapid rise in the birth rate since 1956. Between 1965 and 1970 the primary school population is expected to rise by about 695,000 compared with a rise of about 160,000 over the previous five years. In addition, largely as a result of the trend towards more children staying on at school voluntarily after age 15, the number of senior pupils is expected to rise by about 109,000. To meet the increase in the school population another 29,000 teachers will be needed by 1970 to maintain present staffing standards. Teacher recruitment policies for this period need also to look further ahead to prepare for a continued rise in the school population during the 1970's, which will be accelerated by the raising of the school leaving age. (Department of Education and Science 1965, p. 2)

The education system deals with two kinds of personnel —children and adults. The total numbers in these categories and their relative sizes have important consequences for both the functioning of the institution and the outside society. For example, when teachers are 'overworked' they may be forced into kinds of educational practice which are harmful both to the children and to themselves. The children may then leave school to become parents with attitudes towards education which seriously affect their own children's potentialities for benefitting from education.

To simplify a very complex process we can see that there are several elements in the balance between young and old in schools. Firstly the birth rate in each year decides, with immigration and emigration, how many children are to be included in the education system. Within the minimum number of years for compulsory school attendance there is plenty of space in any series of ten years for wide variation in the yearly cohorts. The actual number of adults in each of the relevant age groups matters in so far as they provide the human raw material from which the teaching force is constructed, but socio-cultural factors which encourage men and women to become and remain teachers are very much more important.

The number of entrants to Colleges of Education will depend in the first place upon the numbers of potential students left over after the universities have filled their places. Secondly, the knowledge and values relating to teaching as a profession will also influence the decisions to use the training once it has been undergone. That the decision to use training is an important and not a marginal factor is supported by the fact that 25% of the men students completing a graduate teaching qualification at one British university in a recent year did not enter teaching in the following year.

The second basic element, then, is the value system. This produces formal prescriptions about the rôles of teacher and student and rules about the minimum leaving and maximum beginning age. In addition, many informal prescriptions of the normative order affect the pupil-teacher balance. For example, there is a strong movement towards 'staying-on' at school beyond the minimum leaving age. This trend provides an interesting example of the connections between the organisation and its normative environment. Regulations governing the calculation of head teachers' salaries reflected the current disparity of prestige between the different kinds of school. They give very many more 'points' per child above the school leaving age. Designed to give grammar school head teachers extra prestige, they also had the unintended consequence of acting as an incentive to secondary modern head teachers who encourage their fifteen-year-olds to stay at school. Significantly, the unintended consequence has been recognised and maintained in the most recent salary structure for headmasters.

As society develops we can expect an inevitable increase in demand for education. Raising the school leaving age will further raise the informal prescriptions in society. We are clearly committed, that is, to a circle of cause and effect between the formal and informal prescriptions about school leaving age which seems certain to have us talking about compulsory education for the over eighteens by the turn of the century. At that point we will have caught up with California in the mid 1960's.

Another aspect of the informal norms which give social reality to the balance in numbers of teachers and pupils are the ideas we have about the pedagogically permissible ratio of pupils to the teacher in the classroom. Teachers have fought an attempt to provide them with auxiliaries to help in classroom organisation and small group work. They are also less than whole-hearted in supporting the development of mechanical aids to teaching. Nevertheless, the enormous possibilities of computerised teaching must surely become a reality in the next half century. Consequently the convention view that 'a class' should consist of 20–45 pupils in the same small room for 'periods' of 40 minutes will disintegrate under the influence of school administration and classroom research. It seems likely that vastly differing group sizes and organisational structure are suited to different aspects of teaching subject matter. For example, a group of five hundred could satisfactorily watch a scientific experiment or Shakespearian play on television. A similarly large number could work through a series of 'frames' in a mathematics course, each student having direct access to the computer which checks his answers and reorganises the questions when he is wrong. We can expect, therefore, that developments in team teaching methods will radically alter the ideal pupil-teacher ratio in people's minds.

The demographic environment of education, therefore, is not simply the age and sex structure of the population. Because personal decisions by both pupils and teachers play a part in determining the mixture of personnel and clients to be found in different parts of the system at different times, we have to take account of the normative order. It affects the proportions of an age cohort who stay at school and the numbers of teachers prepared to face them. Finally it helps to decide attitudes towards the suitability of the current balance and hence the attempts made to alter it.

The administrative environment

Educational aims are an inevitable source of conflict between people in the institution and between them and members of the wider society. Consequently, society has to devise means for controlling the educational system. At the formal level it happens through the operation of local and national government, the churches and other voluntary bodies. It also happens in a way best described by pointing out that the incumbents of the status positions in the educational system are also products of the wider society. That is, they will inevitably carry in their own heads those aspects of the wider normative order which they see to be applicable to the performance of their rôle. Consequently we can never assume that the school is separate from society—it is run by society's own fifth column. Because this 'organic' aspect of the educational system is fairly obvious we can spend more time on analysing the formal control of education.

In the formal aspect of control the Local Authority has a certain kind of right to influence what goes on in school through its control of spending. Most importantly it is responsible for the siting and building of schools, their suitability for the educational process, the allocation of teachers and pupils amongst them and the amount of money which is to be spent by teachers in performing their rôles. The result is a great deal of influence over what goes on in school.

There has been no British sociological research into the consequences of administrative regime upon the educational process. There are, however, a series of elementary pointers towards the consequences of Local Authority

Administration for *some* educational functions. For example, decisions about school-, teacher- and grant-provision in each Local Education Authority are responsible to an important extent for the enormous variation in the proportion of the relevant age group entering higher education. According to the Robbins Report (Ministry of Education 1960) this ranged from 25% in Cardiganshire to less than 2% in West Hampshire. In the areas where the pupil-teacher ratio was below 1:20, 11·3% of the age-group went on to higher education. In contrast, amongst those Local Education Authorities where the secondary pupil-teacher ratio was greater than 1:23 only 6·9% of the age-group entered higher education.

Clearly the pupil-teacher ratio is influenced by decisions made within the administrative environment of the school. In the widest sense it depends upon decisions about teacher salaries and quotas. Closer to the schools, however, the efficiency with which the Local Authority recruits, distributes and supports its teacher force within the framework of administrative possibilities has an incontestable influence upon what happens in the school and consequently what comes out of it. (Eggleston 1967)

The family

Socialisation is one of the inevitable products of social living. Therefore it has many settings; but the family is the most important one. As with the other settings, each family has its own normative order and its regular patterns of behaviour. Its function is to prepare the child for the larger world. Looked at from this point of view, the parents are sponsors of the child with the responsibility of preparing it for adult life. In the process it teaches the child aspects of the normative and behaviour patterns to be found in the wider society. Which aspects these will be depends upon the position of the family itself in the social structure. They will depend, that is, upon the ideas and ways of living which are 'available' to the particular family. These, in turn, stem from the position of the family in the stratification system. Parents can only deliberately teach what they *know*; what they know depends upon their own experiences in society; and their experiences tend to be determined by the amount of money, prestige and power they can command. It is also much more complicated than that. For example, a family with an attachment to a particular religion will include aspects of it in its 'way of life' and consequently in the images of their own family developed by its members. Similarly, the ethnic and other subcultural segments of society will contribute many more distinguishing characteristics to any single family.

In acting as an intermediary between the child and the wider society the parent is not an impartial sieve but a heavily biased selector of experiences for the child. In their decisions about where the family should live, how it should spend its money, which newspapers it takes and political party it supports, parents are limiting and directing the possibilities for social development of the child. This is done deliberately on the basis of the values they themselves have learned in society and accidentally in so far as the consequences of their actions as experienced by the children were not intended. For all these reasons, the child will learn some patterns of behaviour, perceptions of reality and habits of thinking which are features of the wider social environment and some which are special to his family.

So far we have concentrated upon a description of the family as a single unit—as a culture which is an amalgam of elements from the wider culture. Instead of emphasising this cultural aspect we might also see it as a *social system* —as a structure of *status positions* to which are attached expectations of behaviour.

Each individual is linked to the others in ways which are unique to that family. A particular child's problems in coping with conflicting *rôle-prescriptions*—for example between his rôle as a boy-friend and his rôle as a son— will have to be 'solved' by behaviour within this system. The patterns of behaviour thus formed will respond to, and affect, what is going on in school. For example, sex-rôle expectations within the family will influence the responses a child makes to the teacher and the formal rules which he personifies.

'The Family' is a concept. It is either an ideal picture of a vital unit in society which we cherish and aim towards in our own lives or it is a sociological abstraction which is used to help us arrange information about society. In the second use of the term the family has changed over the years as technological, economic and religious change, intensified by recent social crises like the world wars and depressions, have made their impression. Ernest W. Burgess (1948) suggested that six trends could be identified in North America, and all seem to apply to the family in Britain.

Firstly, he emphasised its growing modifiability, adaptability and instability as it responds to the increasing rate of social change. Only the third of these characteristics is in dispute for Britain. It has been argued that the family is no less stable than it used to be—the difference being that it used to break up for different reasons. Most importantly, the family was much more likely to be 'broken up' by the death of a parent than is now the case. (Fletcher 1966, Musgrove 1966) Whether one wishes to see the increasing divorce-rate as a sign of social health or ill-health there is no disputing the fact that it has important consequences for what goes on in school. Similarly, the changing morality of family behaviour has its influence upon the adolescent. He or she, in turn, places strain upon the educational system, particularly when its personnel are striving to maintain the established order as they knew it a generation previously.

Secondly, increasing *urbanisation* of life is a primary characteristic of change. Urbanisation can mean many things, but if we take America as a model it appears to mean two things that are vitally important to the education system. Firstly, it seems to intensify the process of segregation according to income and race. The educational problems which this is causing in the major cities of the United States are stupendous and there is every sign that they will be followed on a smaller scale in Britain. If allowed to proceed without control there is a real prospect that social divisions will be intensified. Communities can become isolated from the remainder of society, developing sub-cultures in which poverty and psychological *alienation* reproduce themselves in each succeeding generation.

Secondly, urbanisation appears to exacerbate social problems to the extent that space is not used according to human needs. In simple terms, the journey to work lengthens and becomes a greater strain, centres of leisure activity move further away and the use of space for recreation is disorganised. Such a situation allied to the growing segregation of sub-cultural groups based either on race or on the lack of ability to move out, produces an environment in which traditionally organised education becomes increasingly pointless.

Whilst it is obvious that counteracting the social problems is partly an educational problem—to teach people the cognitive skills, values and motivations which will permit them to do something about their plight—the situation in the community and wider society can be such as to prevent success. If, for example, a particular community suffers from inadequate housing, the education system tends to become simply a rescue service—giving very small numbers of selected children a chance to move out. In problem areas such as these the system of education has to become one division of an army participating in a co-ordinated attack upon the core problems. It has recently shown itself to be willing in spirit when the Plowden Report (Department of Education and Science 1967) proposed a scheme for Educational Priority Areas in which intensive and unconventional attempts will be made to counteract the effects of urbanisation.

Within the family, changes in the division of labour are certain to occur with the changes in outside normative and action patterns. Burgess argued that as the division of labour in the family loses its extrinsic functions like 'economic production, education, religious training and protection' there will be a change in emphasis which concentrates upon 'the giving and receiving of affection, bearing and rearing of children and personality development.' Consequently he predicted increasing companionship based upon democratic relations which derive from common interests, concensus and democratic association. Since this kind of family situation has been found to associate with achievement in school it becomes possible to expect that the general level of ability to do school work will improve.

Talcott Parsons used these ideas in pointing to a single aspect of the social process which plays a crucial part in what has been happening to the family in modern industrial society. He suggested that the key to understanding

71

F

family changes lies in the concept of *differentiation*, that is, increasing specialisation enables individuals and groups to concentrate upon more detailed and intensively performed tasks. This is true for social living as it is for economic production. Therefore, the family becomes more specialised in its functions.

As part of this differentiating process the nuclear (two generation) family has become separated from the remainder of its wider family in both geographical and economic ways. Industrialisation requires individuals as economic units rather than families and it requires them to be mobile. In the same way many of the older functions of the family have been usurped by other institutions. Financial, medical, social and socialisation activities have at least partially been taken over. The family is not only left with fewer functions to perform but increased opportunity to do them well. Thus, 'the family is more specialised than before, but not in any general sense less important, because of certain of its vital functions.' (Parsons 1956, pp. 10–11)

Many social observers argue that increasing differentiation involves 'fragmenting' the lives of its members. In doing so it reduces their chances for close contacts with other human beings, thereby accentuating social problems. Parsons, on the other hand, looked to the increasing freedom it offers. The individual has greater opportunity to become more human by developing his own powers.

It will be a long time before sociologists agree upon the accuracy of the observations about what is actually happening to the family. It will be even longer before we all agree about whether or not they are good, but the implications of both kinds of argument for the study of education are clear.

Social class

Many studies have shown that social class influences the ways in which children participate in the formal system of education. Wide differences in 'class chances' for education were recognised by social observers prior to the Second Word War, but the egalitarianism behind the 1944 Education Act encouraged us to develop a misleading picture of educational opportunity which lasted for a decade.

Explanations for the deep and stubborn differences in 'class chances' can be found at many different levels. Within teaching folklore we learn that children who do the best work are easiest to control and stimulate, make the best prefects, stay at school longest, take part in extra-curricular activities and get the best references, tend to come from middle class homes. At this level of explanation they get the best chances because they are more teachable. Middle class children do better in the school selecting process because they are that much better at doing the tests which are relied upon in school as the fairest hurdles. Such a perspective also encourages us to believe further that this is so because they are also innately superior to the working class children as well as having had the benefits of the more 'stimulating' home environment of the middle class family.

The sociological level of explanation pays more attention to the fairly obvious fact that the level of collective ability of a nation is a function of its culture. That is, the way a society organised itself, the intellective, value, and motivational demands it makes of its members and the perceptions of reality it teaches, all produce in its people their ability to cope with their own environments.

73

In the light of these ideas sociologists suggested that the startling differences in ability of children from different social classes were proof of sub-cultural variation in preparation for the social life of the school. Certain of the ways in which this preparation matches up with the requirements of the social life of the school are 'measured' in the minds of teachers and add up to perceptions of what they call ability.

Getting on in school, then, is a matter of social evaluation and social evaluation depends upon previous experience. For fairly obvious reasons we can expect that much previous experience will be based upon the social class structure. The most important of these reasons will be the traditional association between the system of education and the middle class. A particular education has tended to be a hallmark of middle classness and the virtues upon which the institution is founded are those of established 'respectable' society. To some extent school is another way in which higher classes can sponsor the access to 'life-chances' of entrants from the lower classes.

Apart from this simple connection we have to push deeper into the ways in which sub-cultural experience produces the cognitive, cathectic and evaluative equipment of the child. In fact, we can say a great deal about the content of life in the different social classes and there is good reason for believing that some aspects matter very much to educational adaptation. One of the most useful approaches employs the set of categories which Florence Kluckholn (1967) recommends as a way of analysing the *implicit culture* or 'ethos' of a group. She suggests that every culture contains, implicitly, some kind of answer to each of several basic questions about the environment. That is, within the life of the group it is possible to discern certain 'truths' which are accepted by all and not subject to violent changes because the members are unaware either of their existence or of possible alternative answers. These truths she terms *life orientations*.

For example, the time-span of attention to the world is clearly very different in the different social classes. In our ideal type we must characterise lower class life as containing an immediate orientation. Things happen now. We can think about tonight and perhaps towards the weekend or job-end but the future is too nebulous a concept to carry a great deal of influence. In contrast the ideal-type middle class life is future-orientated. It is founded upon a time-span of attention which can cover generations. *Deferred gratification* for the sake of future benefits is the keystone of life.

An aspect of the 'instrumental' approach which middle class life tends to produce is the orientation to action which sees it as accomplishing tasks. In contrast the lower class orientation tends to see action as experience and experience as the justification of action. Accomplishing tasks is also seen to be the object of individual intentions and responsibility. Such a view is much less widespread in the lower classes where many individual accomplishments are seen to be much less achievable. It is perhaps less valid to transfer Kluckhohn's description of American middle class life as individualistic rather than familistic in its orientation to social relationships in Britain. But, as far as the needs of educational adaptation are concerned it is probably reasonable to argue that the kinds of individualistic and familistic approaches to social relationships engendered in middle class life, help rather than hinder adaptation. Like so much of our folklore knowledge about education whether they do or not still remains to be shown.

However, with this model of the two ideal-types of social class sub-cultures we have the beginnings of a description of how different social class experience produces different cognitive, cathectic and evaluative skills and habits.

If this profile is at all accurate, it gives us valid grounds for assuming that the lower class member will tend to learn attitudes and actions which assume that nature cannot be logically analysed and manipulated over a long period of time by independent individual action. For many reasons, not the least of which is the kind of language they learn, they tend to develop notions about how the world around can be influenced, which add up to a kind of subjugation on their part. In contrast, middle class members learn to look upon the physical and social environment as a structure to be manipulated. They learn to assume that the mechanism works in explicable, predictable ways. Influencing it is only a matter of finding what had produced the situation to be dealt with and taking appropriate action. On the other hand, the lower class expectations of the environment make room for a very much greater element of luck, coincidence and unpredictability. The world around us is less like a structure which can be manipulated than an amorphous series of events and actions to which one might respond in an immediate and personal way but which one cannot expect to control. The consequences in educational adaptiveness are fairly obvious. To the extent that the school demands suppression of spontaneity, deferred gratification and an instrumental approach to the world around it will tend to find lower class pupils unsuitable.

The peer group

The process of socialisation continues throughout life as the individual encounters an ever-widening circle of groups into which he must be initiated. One of the first groups which is genuinely outside the family is formed by his age-peers.

A useful paradigm for analysing the consequences of group membership will illuminate the effects of this inter-action between school and peer group. (Cole 1962, p. 119)

In the first place a group can be identified by the fact that its members share a common culture in so far as it bears upon the activities of the group. Groups, therefore, are carriers of culture. The normative and behavioural order of the peer group will make demands upon the child when he is performing rôles within it and within other groups. Adaptation to one or other group is likely to suffer where these demands conflict with the rôle prescriptions of the school. If an attitude towards authority expected of a boy in a gang is different to that expected by his teacher either his prestige in the eyes of his peers or the view his teacher has of him must change.

Groups stimulate their members. Two people can have an effect upon each other which will be the greater for the fact that they share common definitions. The group situation is also capable of producing intensive pressures upon the individual to force him into activities of which he would otherwise be incapable. Similarly, cross-group tensions will make demands of individuals which lead them to change their behaviour.

Apart from stimulating, groups also control the action of their members. This is another way of looking at the within-group stimulation of the individual. There is no need to repeat the discussion of the power of the normative order and the social sanctions which lie behind it. From the point of view of the teacher the need for an accurate appraisal of the peer group surrounding each individual member of his class is often paramount. Without it he is unaware of one of the major forces controlling their action.

Groups also isolate their members. They do this through the behavioural patterns based upon the normative order or by developing cognitions of the environment suited to the culture of the group. In many ways, therefore, the culture of the peer group works to insulate its members from the influence of the school. For example, a peer-group rejection of academic values and an emphasis upon sport, social attitudes or fashion, tends to put the life of the school beyond the pale for its members. This does not mean that nothing is learned or that ex-members of a particular gang or peer group cannot regain an interest in school-work. Nevertheless, the peer group in responding to, and influencing, the social establishment of the school can engender new attitudes and personality states. Conflict with the school over a period of time may have important consequences for the developing personality and for its future chances in life. But, a school can also support an adolescent through his membership of a youth group in such a way as to minimise its deleterious effect upon educational and occupational opportunities. Unfortunately, it is one of the problems of the educator that the same school structure has a differential effect upon its clients. Different pupils within it will perceive it as being undemanding, conflicting or tolerant in this respect.

Groups can also have therapeutic value for their members. This is equally likely for the child in the peer-group. If a peer group maintains a sense of self-respect and self-confidence it can preserve a potentially successful person from the effects of 'failure' in school. The experience of group life may also relieve tensions and anxieties while providing affection and a sense of 'belonging' if the necessary figures are missing from the young person's life outside the peer group. Our society manages to combine a strong concern for prestige with a strictly limited structure of opportunities for its acquisition. In that situation small groups will often reduce the sense of failure an individual might otherwise develop.

Finally, groups make for effective effort and accomplishment by channelling co-operative group effort into the achievement of group goals. The ability to make use of this power of group cohesion is a vital part of the stock in trade of the successful teacher.

These are the functions of all groups for their members but peer groups have special characteristics and functions of their own. One of the least understood, but most important, functions of the peer group is to assist the parents in their primary responsibility—that of fitting the child for life outside the family group and independent of it. As the child grows up he encounters socialisation from a widening circle of groups in which the peer group occupies a crucial position as a 'buffer state' between the security of the family and the many large and impersonal groups to which he must adapt as an adult. Because it is small, the family can offer experience in only a portion of the various social relationships needed in modern society.

Somewhere he must also learn to carry out the more specific and formal rôles with the low degree of *affectivity* required by modern society. Peer group life provides opportunities for experience in a range of such rôles which is different to, and a complement of, those to be found in the family. Often, of course, they will tend to be merely an extension of the family situation—a child who dominates in the family may find himself dominating a peer group—but it need not be so, and even where it is we can expect some widening of rôle experience. Rather more subtly, the experience of peer group membership helps to break down the childhood views which accept family orientations to the world as *the* orientations.

The peer group is an introduction to adulthood in other ways for it also has an important bearing upon patterns of adult association. Most people choose their marriage partners through peer group connections and consequently the peer group can act as both a restrictor and a broadener of social horizons and of actual opportunities. Within the context of opportunity-structure, the actual education system must be given a high importance. A great deal of research has emphasised the strong influence which the peer group can have upon motivation to achieve in education. Most importantly, it tends to work towards raising an adolescent's sights when they are set below his group norm without depressing them when they are above it.

So far, the discussion of the peer group has concentrated upon the small group situation—a schoolboy and his friends. But this is only the immediate context of a much wider peer group culture which must also be looked upon as a powerful factor in determining what goes on in school. Variously known as 'teensville', 'the fun culture' or 'the land of the young pretenders' it has earned itself an enviable ability to terrify the older generation in most western societies.

In Britain, the situation has led some observers to describe the conflict between the generations as the major split in society. It is not at all difficult to counteract such fears by evidence of the extent to which adolescents resemble their elders. It is also conceivable that the fun culture of teenage life is only a reflection of deeper social class conflicts resulting from our failure to produce a system of educational and occupational opportunity more commensurate with the needs of an advanced industrial society. Nevertheless, the presence of the culture is plain.

One researcher has argued that teenage culture represents

a deliberate revulsion from the middle class values of responsibility and self-discipline. It is a working class manifestation which honours spontaneity and self-expression. This culture is clearly linked with a rejection of the academic rat-race as adolescents turn to immediate gratification with clothes, 'indisciplined' behaviour, and pop music fashions.

> Present teenage culture has developed over the last decade into a complex celebration of many of the values rooted in working class experience, centred around trouble, toughness, smartness, fate and excitement. Far from disappearing, working class culture has been transformed to meet adolescent needs and tastes. Its appeal cuts across class lines, but its impact is mainly on the working class adolescent. (Downes 1966)

From the educator's point of view the crucial point is that there are social class differences in the extent to which an adolescent can survive the youth culture. In the bad old days it was 'the rich what gets the pleasure and the poor what gets the blame'! Nowadays the adolescent fun culture is something which both working and middle class children enjoy but which the former tend not to survive. For the working class child it is 'real' life which requires not only an attitudinal, but also a practical rejection of the educational mobility ladder.

Conclusion

Sociologically speaking a person or a social group has an environment comprising the patterns of action and the cognitions, cathexes and evaluations to be found among the people who surround it. This person or the members of this group interacts with these surrounding patterns as he or they understand them. How the patterns are grouped in an analyst's mind will depend upon the questions he hopes to answer and the configurations which appear to be empirically present.

In analysing the environment of the institution of education several models have been employed. In British research and writing the concept social class has played a predominating rôle usually in an attempt to summarise all aspects of child-, teacher-, school- or institutional environment.

5

The social functions of education

The basic dual function

Each person is prepared by society for future life within it.
However trite this statement may be it contains the basis
for analysing the functions of education. The school system
is a deliberate attempt to maintain the normative and action
patterns of society by influencing its new entrants. In any
society there is an interplay between the normative and
behaviour patterns and the school is often forced to play
the rôle of referee in maintaining values while facing the
realities of actual behaviour.

Schooling and consensus

We have said that the school system has to reflect and
stabilise society. What do we mean by this? Clearly, there
is nothing unsound about the idea that society makes
special provision to see that change is not too rapid. But
what is this society which the school is trying to reflect?

We then begin firstly to enter a debate about the reality of culture and secondly a debate about the usefulness of such a mode of analysis when applied to the rapidly changing, diversified industrial society.

The 'inculcation of culture' idea has now become more complicated because of the need to consider what we mean by culture. We have then to make it even more complicated by relating it to the methods by which the school will carry out the inculcating. Does it aim to teach a given picture of the culture as truth or does it aim to develop ability and initiative to explore culture? As a matter of fact, the former method is likely to take precedence in slowly changing societies where all living generations and those within memory have had basically similar experiences and cultural explanations for them. Clearly, also, the rapidly changing societies must tend in the other direction. The school is now preparing children for cultural situations which it cannot adequately foresee. It must concentrate therefore upon preparing the pupil with tools (techniques and values) for handling unknown situations.

The second kind of problem is special to large, diverse and rapidly changing societies. It is so great that some sociologists doubt the value of using 'socialisation into culture' as a conceptual model for analysing education.

> The sociology ... interprets the relation of education either psychologically, to mean that education makes its contribution to social cohesion through the formation of the 'basic personality', or ideologically, through the inculcation of an appropriate set of common values. Yet it seems doubtful whether this notion of 'integration' can be applied to the ramified, complex structures of modern industrialised societies. In any case, it is clearly easy to exaggerate both the actual and the possible con-

tribution of formal educational institutions to consensus in these societies, whether we think in terms of the formation of basic personality or of the inculcation of a common set of values. It need hardly be said that the importance of schools and universities as agencies of socialisation in relation to the social class and occupational structures, and thus their contribution to a shambling sort of social integration, is not in doubt; but what are we to understand by consensus in these societies? (Floud and Halsey 1959, p. 293)

Thus, the problem lies in the usefulness or otherwise of the idea that modern society has a consensus—they point rather to the diversity of norms, values and behaviour that goes into the many different communities in our society. But how are we to square this warning with those from other observers who complain about the growth of a mass society in which all our values and behaviour have been homogenised by the mass media into a suet-pudding society of standardised everything? It is also possible that consensus need not mean simply that all the members of the society have the same values. Instead we might be able to say that it occurs when the members of society agree that the values of other members of society are acceptable even where they are different. If the members of society are satisfied with their lot and the structure of society that has decided it for them, we have a kind of consensus. It is not one which depends upon widespread holding of a whole series of values, but upon widespread agreement over a single basic one. In the days when the school day ended in a prayer that The Lord should keep us in our proper station education was being used to maintain consensus by encouraging people to accept their differences.

Even if it is too difficult to make out a case for education as a major determinant in consensus we would still wish to use the model in analysing the process of education. Firstly, because it is the model in the minds of the personnel involved in the functioning institution—teachers think they are doing this. Secondly, it is highly relevant to the process whereby the school contributes (or otherwise) towards the adaptability of the child to his local community. That is, if we lower our sights from the societal to the community, neighbourhood or social class level we will find that the socialisation perspective can become a crucial one.

Schooling and social change

Education is beginning to look like a conserving institution which can only follow social change and never initiate it. Such an evaluation, however, is not only too pessimistic, it is also poor social analysis. Social science is rapidly outgrowing the need to find monocausal or unidirectional associations between changing institutions or cultural elements. Whatever else it is, society is a system of interacting structures in which each institution has some effect upon the others as well as being influenced by them.

Apart from this, we have had very little evidence upon which we can base any view. For education to have a chance to become a 'prime mover' in social change it needs to be widespread throughout the population, persistent in influencing the individual and it must be linked with the occupational structure in a more than subordinate fashion. It is only recently that this latter requirement has begun to be met. Hitherto, the educational system has been closely tied to the occupational system in the sense that the kind of education a person received was determined by the social class position of his parents. The balance of superordination between the two institutions is becoming more equitable—occupation determines education slightly less rigidly and education determines occupation much more conclusively than previously. Education is thereby gaining a more strategic position for influencing the distribution of power in society.

We have by no means assimilated the consequences of the 1944 Education Act which experimented with the idea of including ALL and ONLY high ability children in a single kind of school and taking over the already existing grammar school for this purpose. Two important consequences have followed from this experiment. Firstly, in conjunction with many other social factors, it produced an upsurge in the national collective ability—it wasted fewer people and it made its pupils more able than they would have been had they received the pre-war type of education. Secondly, partly as a consequence of this fact and the resulting increase in social mobility via the educational ladder, it contributed to its own replacement by a comprehensive system. The belief in equality of opportunity which was enshrined in the idea of 'secondary education for all' caught the tenor of the times, and growing proportions of parents in society saw a real prospect for their children to receive a 'better chance' than they had.

At the same time the more obvious indicators of social stratification (like the ownership of household goods) were being eroded. As a result a perception of social reality began to gain ground which encouraged people to believe that the boundaries between social classes were diminishing. However, in the last few years we have become much more sophisticated in understanding the mechanisms by which a system of stratification maintains itself and realise that it amounts to much more than a set of rules about consumer behaviour (Lockwood 1966). Consequently, two factors have merged to produce a sense of need for greater

87

equality of opportunity. Firstly, research on school and occupational selection has clarified the picture of what actually happens. Secondly, social attitude changes founded partly on the grammar school experiment and partly on economic changes have produced a widespread sense of dissatisfaction with present opportunities. In recognising the place which the educational system can play in achieving our values we have increased our ability to use it as a lever for social change.

Another way of describing the essential factors upon which the power of education depends is to say that it will follow from the extent to which power and prestige is *achieved* rather than *ascribed* in society. Within this tendency, the extent to which education is a means for achieving status will be crucial.

If we can imagine a society in which all members achieve status on the basis of their performance and all the criteria of performance relate to the skills only taught in schools, the power of education to change society is at a maximum. It is reduced to the extent that a society falls short of this state in either respect. Even this mildly complicated picture falls far short of the important variables. The model assumed power to be equally distributed throughout the occupational structure. This is not so, and we have to contend with the fact that there is an increase in power the higher we move up the prestige continuum. Therefore the power of education to change society is weakened by the degree to which criteria other than educational ones are used for assignment to these elite positions.

Since the war there has been an underlying change in attitudes towards education which have manifested themselves in a steady growth in the proportion of the national income devoted to education. It would be easy to fall into a simple Marxist view which explains the growth as a result of the changes in the underlying 'productive base' of society, since for example, the rate of increase does not seem to vary according to the intentions or values of the governing party. It is as though the governing rhetoric has been irrelevant to the undeniable forces of economic and technological change.

There has also been a change in attitudes towards 'staying on' at school and ever-increasing proportions of our young people are receiving support from their families as they face the rigours of advanced secondary education. At the same time, bodies like the Association for the Advancement of State Education have grown up in which middle-class consumers of state education seek ways of supporting what previous generations of their class peers would have regarded as being irrelevant to their own problems—the education of the masses. Educational issues have even become potential vote-winning topics. Finally, it seems to be becoming occupationally respectable for a middle class boy to take up teaching (as opposed to 'school-mastering', which has always been respectable for some kinds of middle class boy). All these changes are evidence of what might be called a change in national attitudes towards education.

Most importantly, the notion that education is a follower of social change is based almost entirely upon historical observation of education which was not manifestly aimed at bringing about serious social change—only to ameliorate small problems like the need to 'educate our masters', i.e. to teach the electorate those things which the establishment wished them to know. It is, therefore, perfectly reasonable to argue that educational change has not brought about serious social change while holding a belief, based upon evidence of the consequence of educational change, that properly used it has the power to become an instrument for social change.

The functions of the education system

Before describing the functions of education we have to make an important distinction between two ways of describing the consequences of action. One way describes how certain sets of values, or patterns of behaviour actually contribute to the social system of which they form a part and the other concentrates upon the intentions and perceptions of the people who take part in the behaviour. Their intentions and perceptions *may* coincide with the actual result of their actions, but it would be very naïve indeed to assume that they *do*.

The important consequences of an act may or may not be understood by the people who carry it out. Even if they are understood they need not have been their reasons for taking part. It is a commonsense precaution, therefore, to distinguish between societal or community consequences which the individuals intend to follow from their actions and those which eventually do. This is the difference between manifest and latent functions. In either case 'function' relates to empirical truth rather than to the desired ideal of the observer. Specifying functions will, of course, involve description of the participants' desired ideals— these are essential ingredients in the manifest functions of the system. It would be impossible to understand the workings of an institution without taking into consideration what the members believe they are achieving because their actions will depend upon those very beliefs. The manifest-latent distinction is mainly a device for reminding ourselves of the dangers in assuming that intended consequences include all consequences.

There are at least four manifest functions of education in our society. Firstly, it has to inculcate the values and standards of the society. That is, education is designed to develop in children the beliefs, habits of thought and of action which are thought to be necessary and desirable in society. Secondly, it has to maintain social solidarity by developing in children a sense of belonging to the society together with a commitment to its way of life as they understand it. Thirdly, it has to transmit the knowledge which comprises the social heritage. Fourthly, it is also expected to develop new knowledge.

The latent functions are the unintended consequences for society of the institution. People may not take part in religious ceremonies in order to strengthen their feelings of solidarity with their group, but that is usually a consequence. Hence it is a latent function of religious observance in that group. Four latent functions of education are fairly obvious but the list is more or less endless. It is a free baby-sitting service, separating children from their parents for regular and reasonably prolonged periods of the day and year. This has important implications for parental responsibility and freedom of action and has wide ramifications through the other aspects of the social structure. Because young adults usually choose their mates from amongst their educational peers it is also a useful marriage market. Similarly, it provides opportunities for children to become acquainted with a wider and more diverse circle of friends than they would otherwise reach. Friendships thus prepared can be important in later social or occupational careers. Finally, it is a means by which the supply of labour is reduced.

In noting latent functions we are not expecting that all members of society will be unaware of their operation. Whether or not a function can be called manifest depends upon the reasons for which the organisations were set up and their current official justifications. The proportion of females who are not aware (to say the very least) of the marriage-market function of higher education is very small. On the other hand, broadening the husband-finding opportunity-structure for the women of Britain does not come high on the list of official justifications for spending money on higher education. However, it is perfectly possible for a latent function to become so obvious and so desirable that it becomes a manifest one. For example, it is not impossible that schooling could be extended for the explicit purpose of reducing manpower supply.

Apart from the general list of functions more specific ones may be drawn up with particular objectives in mind. For example, a foremost educational planner (Anderson 1967) has described five major functions of education according to their contribution to the economic development of society. Schools prepare the child for occupations, widen his participation in the culture from local to national bounds and stimulate his individuality. The fourth and fifth functions he describes societally rather than individually. Schools help to select and mould elites for society. Finally, much of what goes on in them is designed, or serves, to preserve old intellectual systems or introduce new ones.

The difficulty in trying to gather empirical evidence in support of assertions about functions lies in measuring the social changes which are believed to be taking place, apportioning the extent to which education is responsible and the rate at which it is changing. This is made all the more difficult by the fact that functions are often specified at both the individual and the societal level. It is one thing to measure changes in an individual child and something very different to conclude that, for example, if you make some children more creative in certain ways society will become more flexible. At the present time, therefore, statements about functions tend to be a mixture of wishful thinking, personal experience, inferences drawn from data collected for other reasons and simple truisms.

The one area that has received the most attention has been the work of education in preserving the social structure. Even here research has been of a simple head-counting kind which showed how the school distributed access to occupations, insofar as it had the power to do it, according to the already existing patterns of income and prestige. Many people would be prepared to argue that the social class system is fundamental to all that goes on in our society. Consequently, they assume that the subservience of the education system to the social class system is inevitable. There is no need to accept this theory of social change because the empirical evidence for it is neither substantial nor analytically persuasive. However, it is the area which has been best researched so far and for this reason we will start with it.

Schooling and social mobility

Most people think of education as the means by which occupational categories are achieved. They not only think of it this way amongst other ways—as a means for teaching good behaviour perhaps—but such a view tends to predominate. It is what they think of first and if pushed it is what they believe to be the most important consequence of education for their own children.

However crudely one wishes to simplify description of the relationship between schooling and education it will be difficult to do violence to the folklore view. The primary school teacher who forecasts a worthless future as a dustman for a child who is lazy in school is talking a language its parents would understand. Education and occupation are inextricably interwoven concepts in the minds of the general public. It is also an objective fact that education matters to occupational opportunity—the man in the street is not soft—as he might say. As a sociologist would put it, subjective perceptions of opportunity-structures tend to approximate structural features.

From the consumers' point of view, then, the first function of education is to prepare their children for occupational status. This alone has been sufficient justification for the post-war research into the relationship between education and stratification. Since stratification has been shown to be a vital complement of education we must begin to deal with it now.

There is reason to believe that all societies which produce a surplus over the very minimum physiological requirements of its members develop a system of ranking to share out rewards and duties differentially amongst the population. There are many points of view about what social class is, how it comes about, how it is changing as a social and societal phenomenon and how it influences other societal structures. A thorough understanding of these ideas and the data which support them is essential if we are to understand this relationship in all its complexity. However, we can be satisfied at this stage with a preliminary description of the field so that some general associations between formal education and stratification can be pointed out.

Even in modern industrial societies many social class positions are still ascribed but the pace of economic (and hence social) change is so great that new positions are constantly being created which have to be achieved. Upward social mobility is now more or less respectable and with both leaders of the major political parties making discreet use of their own histories of social mobility as points in their favour, there is a possibility that we shall reach the stage which American society reached in the late nineteenth century in which mobility was a genuine (as opposed to an inverted snobbery) reason to be proud of oneself. How the two countries set about organising education and what they believe they are doing has been well described by Ralph Turner (1960) who characterised the British system as one which offered sponsored mobility as opposed to the contest mobility of the American system. Whatever way it is carried out and regardless of what the members of society think they are doing, there is no doubt that there is a fair amount of mobility in both societies. (Lipset and Bendix 1959)

Education is probably an important social mobility 'ladder', although this is by no means as certain as we would expect from the discussions. However, from the point of view of the practitioner in the formal system of education, what really matters is that people in society think it is a main ladder. Pressure upon the school from parents, if not properly prepared for (and made use of) can encourage teachers in the educational-isolationism which looks forward to the time when teaching is the province of initiated 'experts'. In this way the outside social environment of the school has an important influence upon what goes on inside it.

Social mobility may be reduced in its simplest terms to the picture of a child born in one stratum finishing its life in the one above or below it. From the point of view of the individual, the social stratification system can be seen as an opportunity structure. There is before him a set of opportunities for achieving differently valued positions which varies over time depending upon general economic development, migration and redistribution of population as a stratum becomes unable to produce the individuals of sufficient calibre to hold down all the jobs.

In England, the opportunity-structure has remained surprisingly static to the working class man, perhaps because general economic development has worked through its increase in male white-collar jobs. The only other ways in which the structure of opportunities can widen to the manual class is by a failure on the part of the middle class to reproduce itself adequately—if too few middle class children are born. An alternative situation can also be envisaged—that some of the lower white-collar occupations continue their downward drift in status until they reach a point where they must be considered part of the manual category. In this case, movement into those non-manual occupations is no longer part of the opportunity structure to the children of skilled manual workers.

It is a matter of modern folklore that education is an important avenue of mobility. A great deal of research takes this for granted and there are certain ways of arranging the data which gives this impression. 'A man of forty may be judged by his performance in an examination at the age of fifteen. The ticket on leaving school or college is for a life journey.' (Marshall 1953, p. 64.) However, what seems to be a dissonant note has been struck by Gosta Carlsson (1958) who came to the conclusion that 'the factor of education does not come out of the analysis in the impressive manner we might have expected on the basis of the many discussions of its rôle and the keen interest in it as a factor, behind social mobility.'

This is an important consideration for the educationalist who tends to think the opposite, for if Carlsson is correct, we will have to be much more specific in discussing the importance of education for social change. It would, in fact, lend a great deal of support to the suggestion that education is more a blocking agent, reinforcing the existing social situation rather than an influence towards change. Carlsson's main conclusions are (1) that schooling is a great asset to those who have it; but (2) taking the overall picture, it is by no means the major influence in the total upwardly mobile group. This highlights the difference between his approach and that of other writers. Previously, the 'influence of education' has been looked at from the point of view of a single individual. Carlsson's method (later used with similar conclusions on U.S.A. and British data by Anderson (1961)), was to look at the upwardly mobile group as a cohort and describe it in educational terms. Consequently, his results are a function of the very low proportion of individuals obtaining anything but elementary education. The corollary of this is that as the proportion of individuals with higher education increases in society, so the importance of education in the upwardly mobile cohort will increase.

There is no real contradiction in the two points of view. The usual method emphasises the near certainty of mobility to individuals who gain a certain standard of education. But this does not mean that education is the only, or even the most important avenue of mobility in society. Carlsson has drawn our attention to the possibility that people unwittingly make such as assumption. On the basis of information collected about people educated before World War II it would seem that many more people were mobile despite a lack of qualifications rather than because of them.

Looking at society in process, education can still be seen to be the most powerful factor—the cuckoo that, in this society, ousts all others. Of people educated before 1944 there were too few cuckoos. As their number approaches the number of available nests the carnage amongst the other inmates—family or political influence, individual accumulation of capital, bureaucratic promotion, experience, luck, etc.—becomes more obvious. Certainly theoretical writings point in this direction. 'Opportunity to rise in the social and economic scale depends less and less upon the accumulation of small capital, more and more on the possession of degrees and diplomas.' (Banks 1955, p. 240) 'Customary methods of recruitment into industry and of vertical mobility within it are becoming obsolescent.' (Floud 1950, p. 120)

In addition to the increased use of education which depends upon the opportunities open to the members of the society for using it, one must look at the structural changes in society. There are changes which have probably caused the drive for increased provision of education, but which also tend to increase the demand on the part of employers for educational qualifications. They have been well analysed and the conclusions seem unquestionable:

Thus modern industrial societies are distinguished in their structure and development from others of comparable complexity, principally by the fact and implications of the institutionalisation of motivation; that is to say, by the public and private organisation on a large and increasing scale of scientific research in the service of economic and military growth. Their occupational structures are characteristically diversified with relatively high educational qualifications for all employment but the lowest. Education attains unprecedented economic importance as a source of technological innovation, and the educational system is bent increasingly to the service of the labour force, acting as a vast apparatus of occupational recruitment and training. (Halsey 1961a, p. 2)

Education as a sorting and selecting agency

With all the qualifications which have been mentioned so far in this chapter we can say that the formal system of education provides an avenue for social and economic mobility by selecting individuals and allowing them special access to the economy. That it does this is obvious. *How* it does it is the interesting question. Some of the answers (or rather how to ask some of the important questions) were presented in the discussion of education as the production of talent. Another set of questions which throw some light on how the sorting and selecting goes on involves a head-counting approach to the school as an input-output system. We look at what human material goes in and what comes out of the school on certain criteria which we feel to be important and then we assume that the educational system has been responsible. Four functions of selection are to be defined in this way but they should not be looked upon as four mutually exclusive categories which collectively cover all that the education system does for society. They are four perspectives which will provide helpful information and useful insight into its functioning.

'Educational' selection

Anderson's fifth function of education was the preservation of old, and the introduction of new, intellectual systems.

> The schools do this by identifying and producing competence to persist to higher levels of school and by cycling personnel back into the expanding system as teachers. In its higher reaches this cultural function of the schools creates and supports a national 'high culture'

and the competence to share in a world culture whether of diplomacy or science. (Anderson 1967, p. 13)

Whatever else the educational system aims to do, this is probably its most important manifest function. If we are to measure how well it is carrying out this function we will need to specify the criteria according to which the members of the system aim to stimulate and select children. Having done that we can try to describe the extent to which their actual categorising of children matches up with their intentions. In doing so we will be describing the consequences of education in terms of 'educational' criteria. The most all-embracing perspective on the activities of education as an input-output system, therefore, is that which sees it as selecting on educational grounds. In doing so it tries to summarise the beliefs of educators relating to their manipulation of children.

Broadly, they tend to believe that they are choosing or counselling according to a child's ability to meet the requirements of the educational system. In simple terms, a teacher advises a pupil to take 'O' level Latin because he believes that the child has, or will develop, skills and interests which suit him to a particular kind of educational career. This set of beliefs carries with it some very important assumptions. Basically, the counsellors must believe that the requirements of the educational system are sufficiently important to justify such analysis and judgment of children. This requires some combination of four supporting beliefs : —

1. the criteria of ability in the school are relevant to the successful pursuit of 'outside' occupations.
2. educators actually possess the ability to measure potential aptitudes of children.
3. education is irrelevant to the occupational requirements of society.

4. education *ought* to be irrelevant to the occupational requirements of society and we should operate as if it were.

Clearly any single educator's view of education will tend to include elements of all these beliefs. In fact, probably the fairest summary of the common view of education would run something like this. The school's criteria of intellectual and social ability are fairly good indicators of potential for achievement in the occupational sphere and the methods which teachers employ (testing, personal judgements and pupil choice) are fairly efficient measures on the criteria. However, if education falls down a little, firstly in the relevance of its criteria and secondly, in its ability to employ them, it is not very serious because education is also concerned with achieving much less tangible goals like goodness and a sense of justice among its students. This is logically sound provided it can be shown that its deficiency in occupation-preparation and prediction actually do derive from its efficiency in producing and evaluating the less tangible features of personality.

Of the four assumptions the last one is a value judgement and as such is not open to empirical verification. Education is education. If society cannot make 'use' of somebody who has been educated then it is its own lookout and this is a measure of its own deficiency. Education is concerned, that is, with certain ideals which are independent of society. The third is simply wrong and would never be offered as the major assumption. It would only be used as a background to 4—taking the form of an argument that deliberate changes in the existing system will have only minor consequences. The first two assumptions are at the bottom of most educational thought despite the great lack of research behind them. We are in no position at the moment to make categorical statements one way or the other but at least we should be wary of accepting either point. One of the problems of research on, for example, the ability of educators to predict future development of children, is the inevitable operation of the self-fulfilling prophecy described in Chapter II. Prediction itself tends to bring about the consequences it predicts.

Apart from this very serious difficulty in interpreting research, the actual amount of information relating to 'educational selection' as part of the social process is limited. For example, Anderson's third function of education was to stimulate individuality. Obviously, the education system does this to the extent that it breaks down the dependence of an individual upon traditional knowledge and the behaviour patterns of his family and local community. But this is nothing more than a simple truism and we have no idea of how important the result is to society or to individual pupils and we do not know whether the effect is changing. The collection and analysis of data relating to the belief-systems which centre upon these major assumptions of the educational system is the task of the sociology of education since they lie at the heart of the functioning of the system as an institution of society. Everything in this book has a bearing upon this fundamental problem.

Labour force preparation

A perspective upon educating children which is particularly applicable to a current interest in education is one which sees schooling as a way of preparing the children to enter the different occupations in the numbers and with the preparatory skills which are demanded (at both the manifest and latent level) by the economic system. The point is that education mainly influences the development of the economy through its effects upon the social, physical and intellectual skills of its products—the children. As educational provision becomes more widespread and industry becomes more complex in its demands, education takes on an increasingly important rôle in determining the rate and direction of economic change. There have been several attempts by economists to measure the value of education in economic growth and their conclusions have to be viewed sceptically. Nevertheless, the view is spreading that 'the development of educated people is the most important capital formation, their number, quality and utilisation the most meaningful index of the wealth producing capacity of the country.' (Drucker 1959, p. 120)

The Director of the Analysis Division of the UNESCO Social Sciences Department (UNESCO 1964) has summarised some of the ways in which the manpower selection and training function of education serves society:

1. The direct economic impact of education is upon the quantity and quality of occupational skills, labour usually accounting for some three quarters of national output, and education being a major source of the productivity of labour. . . .

2. . . . The educational system can also serve as an instrument of selection by which a society finds its leaders, entrepreneurs, administrators and technicians and improves their quality. (op. cit., p. 18)

The manpower selection function of education, therefore, is one which, if measured, will tell us a great deal about the consequences of education. It will not tell us *all* of course. Trying to measure this function is not the same as assuming that economic production is the sole criterion of good education—only that it is an important one. To do it properly we need to measure over time the output of particular individuals with particular kinds of skills.

H

This can be compared with the manpower requirements at the same periods. A flow chart would then show whether or not education was filling the gaps between requirements and output.

The information on the manpower selection function of education which we gain in this way will have several weaknesses if we are thinking of it as part of a programme of human resource development. First, forecasts of manpower needs cannot be made for anything longer than five year periods and these are much too short for the needs of educational planners who have to think in fifteen to twenty-year periods. Second, and probably more importantly, the desired educational content of particular occupations change over time as knowledge increases and the general standard of education improves. Consequently. the planning process which is carried on by juggling 'counters' like engineer, teacher, carpenter, etc. can be upset by the simple fact that what goes into the 'counters' has changed.

Despite the difficulties and dangers in making use of this perspective to measure the consequences of education, it is the area receiving the greatest attention and it is reasonable to expect that it will pay the greatest dividends in improved ability to enhance the 'freedom, dignity and worth of the individual.' (UNESCO 1964)

Meritocratic selection

Apart from the 'success' of the formal system of education in differentiating children upon its own educational criteria and in relation to the manpower needs of society, two other forms of selection can be attributed to it. The concept of 'meritocratic' selection derives from a notion that access to the most important, most prestigeful and best paid occupations in society should be reserved for the most intelligent. As we saw earlier, it is generally accepted that in our developing society, the educational system is replacing the other avenues of social mobility. Because of this, it is assuming a more and more strategic position for carrying out the function of a sieve of 'ability', distributing occupational rewards according to its definitions of intellectual merit.

We have already dealt with the whole range of abilities which are valued in the system of education in discussing 'educational' selection. Meritocratic selection goes a little further in specifying the criterion upon which the children are deliberately or accidentally sorted. We are concerned with 'intelligence'—only one of the criteria included in 'educational' selection. It is one of the educator's aims in the same way that he aims to make the most of a child's creativity or of his ability to have experiences of the kind which the teacher values. But this criterion is worth dealing with separately because of the importance it has in the general folklore of education.

A great deal of discussion tends to make assumptions about
  (a) the distribution of potential and actual intellectual talent in society,
  (b) the desired rôle of education as selector of high intellectual ability, and
  (c) the actual rôle of education as a selector of intellectual ability.

In fact, because of the difficulty in interpreting 'intelligence' tests there is nothing like adequate information on any of these theoretically measurable aspects of the differentiating function.

An improvement in clarity is offered by Vernon (1957) who distinguished conceptually between intelligence A which is 'some quality of the central nervous system ultimately determined by the genes'; this can be called innate intelligence. Intelligence B is used to represent the exhibiting in everyday life of this innate 'potential' intelligence. Finally, intelligence C may be seen as the samplings of intelligence B which are contained in intelligence tests—the intelligence tests scores. Any discussion about the desirability of opening up university education to more students, or on whether we should 'scrap the $11+$', will carry with it a whole series of beliefs about the different concepts of intelligence and how they are represented in society which are often untenable and conflicting in the light of current knowledge. In order to clarify the issues from the point of view of social differentiation let us take two major 'intelligence' terms and describe how the sociologist would wish to apply them to the description of the sorting and selecting function of formal education.

We can take a popular psychological concern of a decade or so ago as the starting-point in our discussion. Is our national intelligence declining? was a perennial question which showed a primary concern for the potential physiological limits to national talent on the assumption that they have great relevance for the levels of IB and IC. The idea at this time can be summarised rather crudely like a geometrical theorem.

1. the limits of intellectual ability are set by the genetically based central nervous system.
2. the limits are inherited through many genes.
3. 'intelligent' people tend to marry each other.
4. children's intelligence tends towards a level mid-way between that of their parents.
5. 'intelligent' parents have fewer children than those who are less intelligent.

hence: the less intelligent parents produce an increasing proportion of the new generation. Therefore, unless these people limit their families, the average intelligence of the population will decline. It was even forecast that the average level would fall about four I.Q. points in each succeeding generation. (Eckland 1967)

This point of view is tending to be replaced by one much closer to that outlined in chapter III which assumes that the genetic limits to intellectual ability are not specially relevant in the present stage of social development. We expect that a large proportion of the population will have IB's and IC's which are much too far below their IA's for us to talk meaningfully about the innate potential intelligence of the nation on the basis of IC information.

Another of the conventional ideas about ability, education and society is much more important to discussion of the function of education. This is the idea that education picks out people according to their intelligence and directs them towards those occupations in which they are most likely to make their greatest contribution to the society. The statement has to be left as vague as that because people have different ideas of what ability is and about what 'the greatest contribution to the society' is. Frequently the most important (that is, most prestigeful) formulations of this idea mean some mixture of IA, IB and IC. As far as 'contribution to society' is concerned we are usually led to believe that efficiency in the functioning (as opposed to 'quality of life') is meant. One example would be the idea that we cannot afford to have a man who could be an engineer or doctor working as a navvy—'we need all the brains we can get.' We even have a theory of social, industrial or political delinquency which assumes that if a man has to do work below his intellectual ability he will become frustrated and dissatisfied. He will cause trouble of a kind usually thought to be bad for society.

If we are to provide information which can help us to

think more clearly about this function we must make clear the concept of intelligence to be used and then apply it in a 'head-counting' way to the system of education. An attempt has been made to do this (Swift 1965a) which concluded that in two Local Education Authority Divisions the meritocratic function, as measured by IC in relation to grammar school entry (as first step towards high-ability-demanding occupations), reached nearly 70%. That is, 70% of all children who were judged on the criterion of IC to be adequate for grammar school education were admitted to it. One could also put it the other way round—over thirty per cent of all those entitled on the single criterion of IC to make the first important step towards the occupational elite are denied it.

In order to make sense of such information we need to measure the meritocratic selection function of education at all its major points over a long period of time. We would then have a 'flow-chart' showing how efficiency in this respect was changing at each point over time. Alongside such data-collecting we would also need research upon the relationship between IC and the ability to succeed in work. Such evidence as there is on this question suggests that within very broad IC ranges there is no kind of association.

Social class selection

We have seen that education is one of the methods by which society maintains the established order through socialisation. One important aspect of this process is the maintenance of the social class system. Firstly, particular kinds of school can be reserved for children from particular sectors of the population who are then given special access to the occupational structure on the basis of having attended these schools. This is a simplification of a complex self-fulfilling prophecy in which the children of the leaders in society are to become (with other deserving cases) leaders in the future; hence they need special education to prepare them for their future rôles; having undergone this socially superior education they are in fact more suitable for leading rôles in society. The man in the street contributes to this process to the extent that he holds certain assumptions about people of 'quality', the inheritance of ability and the superiority of individuals who exhibit certain characteristics of social behaviour (like accent, confidence in the public eye and a sense of superiority which does not impede subordinate-superordinate relationships).

The second way in which the school contributes to the stability of the social class system is by judging children on the basis of the social characteristics which they bring to school. That is, to the extent that the values, motivations and skills of one social class are represented in the normative and behavioural requirements of the school they will inevitably be employed to evaluate the behaviour of the child. His 'success' will tend to depend upon the social class from which he comes. In this way social mobility is checked.

Many studies have dealt with the school system as a sorter of children on social class criteria. Floud (1956) pointed the way towards this kind of analysis with 11 + selection figures for Middlesborough and South-West Hertfordshire which showed that in 1953 the chance of getting into a grammar school for sons of clerks was four times as great as that for the sons of unskilled workers. At the extremes of the social scale, sons of professional workers have seven times the chance of unskilled workers' sons in Middlesborough and six times as great a chance in South-West Hertfordshire. In such studies it was clear that the lack of balance in 'class chances' was due to the fact that sons of middle class parents were better able to score on intelligence and attainment tests.

On the other hand 'Report on Early Leaving' (Ministry of Education 1954) suggested that there was discrimination on class lines within the same 'ability group' and Douglas (1964) clarified this by showing evidence for a relative deterioration in average working class ability to score on tests between 8 years and 11 years. In 'class chance' analysis we are interested only in the proportions of the different social classes which are given access via the educational system to higher status occupations. One very illuminating example of the usefulness of this approach was given in the Robbins Report. Here we are told that the working class proportion amongst university students has *fallen* from 27% in 1928 to 26% in 1961.

It is figures like these which have to be used to give us an idea of the social class stabilising function which formal education performs. Unfortunately, there is no large work comparable to the Glass study which can provide comprehensive and dependable figures for the present situation. Suffice it to say that the weight of evidence showing bias in class chances is incontrovertible. However, the problem of interpretation still remains because we have nothing with which to compare the extent of bias other than no bias whatsoever or bias at some previous point in time. In the first case the comparison is too unreal to make sense and the second runs the risk of not taking into account changes in society during the period.

Conclusion

In this chapter we have considered several ways in which the consequences of education for society have been analysed. It specifically aimed at moving from the superficial level of discussion about how far education produces social change towards a specification of consequences in empirically verifiable ways. It should not be assumed that this will be an easy victory for clear scientific thinking over woolly and prejudiced impressionism. Even if we were to 'measure' educational manpower, social class and meritocratic selection outputs of the system would we then be in a position to add them together in such a way as to give an acceptable measure of the full contribution which education makes to society?

Bibliography

ANDERSON, C. A., (1960), 'A Skeptical Note on the Relation of Vertical Mobility to Education', *The American Journal of Sociology*, Vol. 66, pp. 560–70.

ANDERSON, C. A., (1966), 'The Impact of the Educational System on Technological Change and Modernisation', in Hoselitz, B. F. and Moore, W. E., *Industrialisation and Society*, Paris: Unesco, pp. 259–78.

ANDERSON, C. A., (1967), *The Social Context of Educational Planning*, Paris: Unesco: International Institute for Educational Planning.

BANKS, O., (1955), *Parity and Prestige in British Education*, London: Routledge and Kegan Paul.

BANKS, O., (1958), 'Social Mobility and the English System of Education', *International Review of Education*, Vol. IV, pp. 196–202.

BARKER, R. G., and GUMP, P. V., (1964), *Big School, Small School: High School Size and Student Behaviour*, Stanford, California: Stanford University Press.

BERNSTEIN, B., (1960), 'Language and Social Clan', *British Journal of Sociology*, XI, 271–276.

BERNSTEIN, B., (1965), 'A Socio-linguistic Approach to Social Learning', *Penguin Survey of the Social Sciences 1965*, Penguin Books, pp. 144–66.

BIDWELL, C. E., (1965), 'The School as a Formal Organisation', in *Handbook of Organisations*, ed. March, J. G., Chicago: Rand McNally, pp. 972–1022.

BLYTH, W. A. L., (1965), *English Primary Education*, London: Routledge and Kegan Paul. Vols. 1 and 2.

BLYTH, W. A. L., (1967), 'Some Relationships between Homes and Schools', in *Linking Home and School*, eds. Craft, M., *et al.*, London: Longmans, pp. 3–13.

BOCOCK, S. S., (1966), 'Toward a Sociology of Learning: a Selective Review of Existing Research', *Sociology of Education*, Vol. 39, pp. 1–45.

BOWMAN, M. J., (1966), 'The Human Investment Revolution in Economic Thought', *Sociology of Education*, Vol. 39, pp. 111–38.

BRAM, J., (1955), *Language and Society*, New York: Random House.

BRIM, O., and WHEELER, S., (1966), *Socialization after Childhood*, New York: Wiley.

BROOKOVER, W. B., *et al.*, (1964), 'Self-Concept of Ability and School Achievement', *Sociology of Education*, Vol. 37, pp. 271–8.

BROOKOVER, W. B., and GOTTLIEB, D., (1964), *A Sociology of Education*, New York: American Book Company.

BURGESS, E. W., (1948), 'The Family in a Changing Society', *American Journal of Sociology*, Vol. LIII, pp. 417–22.

CARLSSON, G., (1958), *Social Mobility and the Class Structure*, Lund: Gleerup.

CASSIRER, E., (1964), *An Essay on Man*, Newhaven, Connecticut: Yale University Press.

CHARTERS, W. W., (1963), 'Social Class and Intelligence Tests', part of section 1, part 1 in Charters, W. W. and Gage, N. L., *Readings in the Social Psychology of Education*, Boston: Allyn & Bacon Inc., pp. 12–21.

CICOUREL, A. V., and KITSUSE, J. I., (1963), *The Educational Decision-makers*, Indianapolis, Bobbs-Merrill.

CLARK, B. R., (1962), *Educating the Expert Society*, San Francisco: Chandler Publishing Company.

CLARKE, B. R., (1964), 'Sociology of Education', in Faris, R. E., *Handbook of Modern Sociology*, Chicago: Rand McNally, pp. 734–69.

CLARKE P. R. F., (1962), 'Complexities in the Concept of Intelligence', *Psychological Reports*, Vol. 11, pp. 411–7.

COHEN, E., (1965), 'Parental Factors in Educational Mobility', *Sociology of Education*, Vol. 38, pp. 404–25.

COLE, W. E., (1962), *Introductory Sociology*, New York: David McKay Company Inc.

COLEMAN, J., (1961), *The Adolescent Society*, Glencoe, Illinois: The Free Press.

CORWIN, R. G., (1965), *A Sociology of Education*, New York: Meredith Publishing Company.

DAVIS, A., (1948), *Social Class Influence upon Learning*, Cambridge, Massachusetts: Harvard University Press.

Department of Education and Science. (1967), *Children and Their Primary Schools*, London: Her Majesty's Stationary Office. [The Plowden Report]

DOUGLAS, J. W. B., (1964), *The Home and The School*, London: MacGibbon & Kee.

DOWNES, D. M., (1966), *The Delinquent Solution*, London: Routledge and Kegan Paul.

DOWNES, D., (1967), 'Decolonising the Young', *The Observer*, 23rd July, p. 7.

DRUCKER, P. F., (1959), *The Landmarks of Tomorrow*, London: Heinemann.

DUBIN, R., (1959), 'Human Relations in Formal Organisations', *Review of Educational Research*, Vol. XXIV, pp. 357–66.

DURKHEIM, E., (1956), *Education and Sociology*, Glencoe, Illinois: The Free Press.

ECKLAND, B. R., (1967), 'Genetics and Sociology: A Reconsideration', *American Sociological Review*, Vol. 32, pp. 173–94.

EGGLESTON, S. J., (1967), *The Social Context of the School*, London: Routledge and Kegan Paul.

EGGLESTON, S. J., (1967), 'Some Environmental Correlates of Secondary Education in England', *Comparative Education*, Vol. 3, pp. 85–97.

ELDER, G. H., (1965), 'Life Opportunity and Personality: Some Consequences of Stratified Secondary Education in Britain', *Sociology of Education*, Vol. 38, pp. 173–202.

ELDER, G. H., (1965), 'Family Structure and Educational Attainment: a Cross-National Analysis', *American Sociological Review*, Vol. 30, pp. 81–96.

ELVIN, H. L., (1965), *Education and Contemporary Society*, London: C. A. Watts & Co. Ltd.

ETZIONI, A., (1961), *Complex Organisations*, Glencoe, Illinois: The Free Press.

ETZIONI, A., (1964), *Modern Organisations*, Englewood Cliffs, New Jersey: Prentice-Hall.

FARBER, B., (1965), 'Social Class and Intelligence', *Social Forces*, Vol. 44, pp. 215–25.

FARIS, R. E. L., (1961), 'Reflections on the Ability Dimension in Human Society', *American Sociological Review*, Vol. 26, pp. 835–43.

FLETCHER, R., (1966), *The Family and Marriage in Britain*, Harmondsworth, Middlesex: Penguin Books.

FLOUD, J., (1950), 'Education and Social Mobility', *Yearbook of Education*, London: Evans Bros.

FLOUD, J., (1962), 'The Sociology of Education', in Welford *et al.*, *Society: Problems and Methods of Study*, pp. 521–40.

FLOUD, J. E., *et al.*, (1956), *Social Class and Educational Opportunity*, London: Heinemann.

FLOUD, J., and HALSEY, A. H., (1958), 'The Sociology of Education', *Current Sociology*, Vol. 7, pp. 165–233.

FLOUD, J., and HALSEY, A. H., (1959), 'Education and Social Structure: Theories and Methods', *Harvard Educational Review*, Vol. 29, pp. 288–96.

FRASER, E., (1959), *The Home Environment and The School*, London: University of London Press.

GLASS, D. V., (1954), *Social Mobility in Britain*, London: Routlegde and Kegan Paul.

GOFFMAN, E., (1959), *The Presentation of Self in Everyday Life*. New York: Doubleday & Company.

GOSLIN, D. A., (1963), *The Search for Ability*, New York: Russell Sage Foundation.

GOTTLIEB, D., (1964), 'Sociology of Education', *Review of Educational Research*, Vol. XXXIV, pp. 62–70.

GOTTLIEB, D., *et al.*, (1966), *The Emergence of Youth Societies*, New York: The Free Press.

GOULD, J., and KOLB, W., eds. (1964), *A Dictionary of the Social Sciences*, London: Tavistock Publications.

GOULDNER, A. W., (1954), *Wildcat Strike*, London: Routledge and Kegan Paul.

GOULDNER, A. W., (1957), 'Cosmopolitans and Locals: Toward an Analysis of Latent Social Roles, II', *Administrative Science Quarterly*, Vol. 2, pp. 444–80.

GRAMBS, J. D., (1965), *Schools, Scholars and Society*, Englewood Cliffs, New Jersey: Prentice-Hall.

GROSS, L., and GURSSLIN, O., (1963), 'Middle and Lower Class Beliefs and Values: A Heuristic Model', in Gouldner, A, and Gouldner, H. P., *Modern Sociology*, New York: Harcourt, Brace and World, pp. 168–77.

GROSS, N., and FISHMAN, J. A., (1968), The Management of Educational Establishments', in *The Uses of Sociology*, eds. Larzarsfeld *et al.*, London. Weidenfeld & Nicolson, pp. 304–58.

HALSEY, A. H., *et al.*, (1961), (a), *Education, Economy and Society*, Glencoe, Illinois: The Free Press.

HALSEY, A. H., *ed.* (1961), (b), *Ability and Educational Opportunity*, Paris: Organisation for Economic Co-operation and Development.

HALSEY, A. H., (1959), Class Differences in General Intelligence I', *British Journal of Statistical Psychology*, pp. 1–4.

HALSEY, A. H., (1967), 'The Sociology of Education', in *Sociology: an Introduction*, ed. Smelser, N. J., London and New York: John Wiley and Sons, pp. 381–434.

HANSEN, D. A., (1963), 'The Responsibility of the Sociologist to Education', *Harvard Educational Review*, Vol. 33, pp. 312–25.

HANSEN, D. A., (1967), 'The Uncomfortable Relation of Sociology and Education', in *On Education: Sociological Perspectives*, eds. Hansen, D. A., and Gerstl, J. E., New York: John Wiley & Sons, pp. 3–34.

HARGREAVES, D. H., (1967), *Social Relations in a Secondary School*, London: Routledge and Kegan Paul.

HAVIGHURST, R. J., (1961), 'Conditions Productive of Superior Children', *Teachers College Record*, Vol. LXII, pp. 524–31.

HIMMELWEIT, H. T., (1966), 'Social Background, Intelligence and School Structure: an Interaction Analysis', in *Genetic and Environmental Factors in Human Ability*, eds. Meade, J. E., and Parkes, A. S., London: Oliver & Boyd, pp. 24–41.

HIMMELWEIT, H. T., (1967), 'The Individual in Society', in *The Educational Implications of Social and Economic Change*, The Schools Council Working Paper No. 12, pp. 13–20, London: Her Majesty's Stationery Office.

HODGKINSON, H. L., (1967), *Education, Interaction and Social Change*, Englewood Cliffs, New Jersey: Prentice-Hall.

HOYLE, E., (1965), 'Organisational Analysis in the Field of Education', *Educational Research*, Vol. VII, pp. 97–114.

HUDSON, L., (1966), *Contrary Imaginations*, London: Methuen.

HUNT, J. MCV., (1961), *Intelligence and Experience*, New York: Ronald Press.

HUSEN, T., (1961), 'Educational Structure and the Development of Ability', in *Ability and Educational Opportunity*, ed. Halsey, A. H., Paris: Organisation for Economic Cooperation and Development, pp. 113–36.

HYMAN, H. H., (1953), 'The Value Systems of Different Classes', in *Class, Status and Power*, ed. Bendix, R., and Lipset, S., pp. 426–42.

JACKSON, B., and MARSDEN, D., (1961), *Education and the Working Class*, Routledge & Kegan Paul.

JACKSON, B., (1964), *Streaming: an Education System in Miniature*, London: Routledge & Kegan Paul.

KAHL, J. A., (1965), 'Some Measurements of Achievement Orientation', *American Journal of Sociology*, Vol. LXX, pp. 669–81.

KEIL, E. T., *et al.*, (1966), 'Youth and Work: Problems and Perspectives', *Sociological Review*, Vol. 14, pp. 117–37.

KLEIN, J., (1965), *Samples from English Culture, Vol. II*, London: Routledge & Kegan Paul.

KLUCKHOHN, F., and STRODTBECK, F. L., (1961), *Variations in Value Orientations*, Evanston, Illinois: Row Peterson & Company.

KLUCKHOHN, F., (1967), 'Variations in Value Orientations as a Factor in Educational Planning', in Bower, E. M., and Hollister, W. G., *Behavioural Science Frontiers in Education*, New York: John Wiley & Sons.

KNELLER, G. F., (1965), *Educational Anthropology*, New York: Wiley

KOHN, M. L., (1963), 'Social Class and Parent-Child Relationships: an Interpretation', *American Journal of Sociology*, Vol, 68, pp. 471–80.

LACEY, C., (1966), 'Some Sociological Concomitants of Academic Streaming in a Grammar School', *British Journal of Sociology*, Vol. 17, pp. 245–62.

LAZARSFELD, P. F., and SIEBER, S. D., (1964), *Organising Educational Research*, Englewood Cliffs, New Jersey: Prentice-Hall

LAZARSFELD, P. F., *et al.*, eds. (1968), *The Uses of Sociology*, London: Weidenfeld & Nicolson.

LIPSET, S. M., and BENDIX, R., (1959), *Social Mobility in Industrial Society*, Berkeley, California: Univeristy of California Press.

LITWAK, E., and MEYER, H. J., (1968), 'The School and the Family: Linking Organizations and External Primary Groups', in *The Uses of Sociology*, eds. Lazarsfeld, P. F., et al., London: Weidenfeld & Nicolson. pp. 522–43.

LOCKWOOD, D., (1966), 'Sources of Variation in Working Class Images of Society', *Sociological Review*, Vol. 14, pp. 249–67.

MALINOWSKI, B., (1947), *Freedom and Civilization*, London: Allen & Unwin.

MARSHALL, T. H., (1953), 'The Nature and Determinants of Social Status', *Yearbook of Education*, London: Evans Bros.

MASLAND, R. L., *et al.*, (1958), *Mental Subnormality*, New York: Basic Books Inc.

MAYS, J. B., (1962), *Education and The Urban Child*, Liverpool: University of Liverpool Press.

MCCLELLAND, D. C., (1961), *The Achieving Society*, Princeton: D. Van Nostrand Co. Inc.

Ministry of Education. (1954), *Early Leaving*, London: Her Majesty's Stationery Office.

Ministry of Education. (1959–1960), *15 to 18: a Report of the Central Advisory Council for Education (England)*. Vols. I and II. London: Her Majesty's Stationery Office. [The Crowther Report]

Ministry of Education. (1963), *Higher Education: a Report of the Committee on Higher Education*, London: Her Majesty's Stationery Office. [The Robbins Report]

MORRIS, B., and SIMMONS, H. W., (1967), 'The School: How do we see it functioning (Past, Present and Future)?' in *The Educational Implications of Social and Economic Change*, The Schools Council Working Paper No. 12, pp. 60–66, London: Her Majesty's Stationery Office.

MORTON-WILLIAMS, R., (1967), 'Survey among Parents of Primary School Children', in Department of Education and Science, Central Advisory Council for Education (England), *Children and their Primary Schools*, Vol. 2, pp. 93–178, London: Her Majesty's Stationery Office.

MUSGRAVE, P. W., (1967), 'Family, School, Friends and Work: a Sociological Perspective', *Educational Research*, Vol. 9. pp. 175–86.

MUSGROVE, F., (1966), *The Family, Education and Society*, London: Routledge & Kegan Paul.

O'BRIEN, R. W., SCHRAG, C. C., and MARTIN, W. T., (1964), *Readings in General Sociology*, Boston: Houghton Mifflin Company.

PARSONS, T., (1956), *Family Socialisation and Interaction Process*, London: Routledge & Kegan Paul.

PARSONS, T., (1959), 'The School Class as a Social System: some of its Functions in American Society', *Harvard Educational Review*, Vol. 29, pp. 297–318.

PARSONS, T., (1961), 'An outline of the Social System', in Parsons et al., *Theories of Society I*, New York: Free Press of Glencoe.

PETERS, R. S., (1967), 'The Status of Social Principles and Objectives in a Changing Society', in *The Educational Implications of Social and Economic Change*, The Schools Council Working Paper No. 12, pp. 28–40, London: Her Majesty's Stationery Office.

SARASON, S. B., and GLADWIN, T., (1958), 'Psychological and Cultural Problems in Mental Subnormality', in *Mental Subnormality*, Part II, R. L. Masland et al., New York: Basic Books Inc.

SCHOFIELD, M., (1966), *The Sexual Behaviour of Young People*. London: Longmans.

SCHOOLS COUNCIL, (1967), *The Educational Implications of Social and Economic Change*, London: Her Majesty's Stationery Office.

SEWELL, W. H., (1961), 'Social Class and Childhood Personality', *Sociometry*, Vol. 24, pp. 340–56.

SHERIF, M., and SHERIF, C. W., (1964), *Reference Groups*, New York: Harper and Row.

SUGARMAN, B. N., (1966), 'Social Class and Values as related to Achievement and Conduct in School', *Sociological Review*, Vol. 14, pp. 287–301.

SUGARMAN, B. N., (1967), 'Involvement in Youth Culture, Academic Achievement and Conformity in School: an Empirical Study of London School Boys', *British Journal of Sociology*, Vol. XVIII, pp. 151–64.

SWIFT, D. F., (1965), 'Meritocratic and Social Class Selection at Age Eleven', *Educational Research*, Vol. VIII, pp. 65–73.

SWIFT, D. F., (1965), 'Educational Psychology, Sociology and the Environment: a Controversy at Cross-Purposes', *British Journal of Sociology*, Vol. XVI, pp. 334–50.

SWIFT, D. F., (1966), 'Social Class and Achievement Motivation', *Educational Research*, Vol. VIII, pp. 83–95.

SWIFT, D. F., (1967), 'Family Environment and 11+ success: some basic predictors', *British Journal of Educational Psychology*, Vol. XXXVII, pp. 10–21.

SWIFT, D. F., (1967), 'Social Class, Mobility Ideology and 11+ Success, *British Journal of Sociology*, Vol. XVII, 165–86.

SWIFT, D. F., (1968), *Reader in the Sociology of Education: an Introductory Analytical Perspectives*, London: Routledge & Kegan Paul.

TAYLOR, W., (1967), 'The Sociology of Education', in *The Study of Education*, ed. Tibble, J. W., London: Routledge & Kegan Paul.

THOMPSON, J. W., (1962), 'Method-Ideology and Educational Ideologies', *Educational Theory*, Vol. 12, pp. 110–7.

TURNER, R. H., (1960), 'Sponsored and Contest Mobility and the School System', *American Sociological Review*, Vol. 25, pp. 855–67.

TURNER, R., (1964), *The Social Context of Ambition*, San Francisco: Chandler Publishing Co.

United Nations Educational, Scientific and Cultural Organisation. (1964), *Economic and Social Aspects of Educational Planning*, Paris: United Nations Educational, Scientific and Cultural Organisation.

VERNON, P. E., (1957), *Secondary School Selection*, London: Methuen.

VERNON, P. E., (1963), 'The Pool of Ability', *The Sociological Review Monograph No. 7: Sociological Studies in British University Education*, ed. Halmos, P., Keele: University of Keele, pp. 45–57.

WARREN, N., (1966), 'Social Class and Construct Systems: Examination of the cognitive structure of two Social Class Groups', *British Journal of Social and Clinical Psychology*, Vol. 5, pp. 254–63.

WHORF, B. L., (1940), *Science and Linguistics*, Vol. XLIV, pp. 229–48.

WILLMOTT, P., (1967), *Adolescent Boys of East London*, London: Routledge & Kegan Paul.

WRONG, D., (1961), 'The Oversocialized Conception of Man', *American Sociological Review*, Vol. XXVI, pp. 183–92.

YOUNG, M., (1965), *Innovation and Research in Education*, London: Routledge & Kegan Paul.

ZNANIECKI, F., (1951), 'The Scientific Function of Sociology of Education', *Educational Theory*, *Vol.* E, pp. 69–78.